Sing a New Song!

Other books by the same author:

Stranger in My Home

The story of transition from the Lutheran to the Adventist ministry. (Nashville: Southern Publishing Association, 1973.)

It's a Two-Way Street

An Adventist theology of preaching. (Washington: Review and Herald Publishing Association, 1978.)

Sing a New Song!

Worship Renewal for Adventists Today

C. Raymond Holmes

Foreword by Norval F. Pease

Andrews University Press

Berrien Springs, Michigan

All Scripture references are from the *Revised Standard Version* unless otherwise indicated by the following abbreviations:
NAS - *New American Standard Version*
NIV - *New International Version*
TEV - *Today's English Version*

Andrews University Press
Berrien Springs, MI 49104

 Published June 1984
Printed in the United States of America

89 88 87 86 85 84 8 7 6 5 4 3 2 1

Library of Congress Catalog Card Number 84-70077
ISBN 0-943872-88-X

Dedicated to Shirley,

my life companion and spiritual foil, who brings to her own Adventist worship experience the deep piety, reverence, and anticipation of her Finnish Lutheran parents, David and Anna Jarvinen.

And whenever the living creatures give glory and honor and thanks to him who is seated on the throne, who lives for ever and ever, the twenty-four elders fall down before him who is seated on the throne and worship him who lives for ever and ever; they cast their crowns before the throne, singing, "Worthy art Thou, our Lord and God, to receive glory and honor and power, for Thou didst create all things, and by Thy will they existed and were created."

Revelation 4:9–11

And they sang a new song.

Revelation 5:9a

Contents

Foreword /

For more than forty years, I have been greatly concerned about the quality of Adventist worship. As a pastor, as a teacher, and as an author, I have tried to encourage worship that is more meaningful and more Christian in its context and form.

At times, I have been tempted to feel discouraged about the witness of our church in this area of concern. In my book *And Worship Him*, I said, "We have published hundreds of books on the *day of worship*, but I don't know of one single Adventist book on the *way of worship*."

I thank God for this book, *Sing a New Song!*, by Dr. Holmes. The author, with his excellent background of training, experience, and skill in communication, has picked up the torch in behalf of better Adventist worship. He has gone far beyond my level of accomplishment in presenting this subject. I consider my work in this field as introductory to Dr. Holmes' deeply profound and highly practical approach.

As you read this challenging book, keep your pencil in hand to underline such sentences as the following:

"There are three distinctive doctrines which ought to be illustrated liturgically in every Adventist church's worship service: the Sabbath, the heavenly ministry of Christ, and the second advent of Christ."

"The Seventh-day Adventist Church . . . is still committed to the centrality of preaching in the worship of God's people."

"The *life*, the *heartbeat*, of the church is worship. Evangelism is the consequence, the natural and powerful outgrowth or result, of the church's worship life. It is the expression of the church's worship extended to the world."

The message of this book is not only for the leader of worship, but also for the worshiper. A thoughtful reading of Dr. Holmes' presentation can bring fresh insight into the unique doctrines of Adventism, a new meaning to the hour of worship, and a new appreciation of preaching and evangelism.

Sing a New Song! has given me deeper insight into the Adventist message and has enhanced my understanding of the place of divine worship in that message. May God bless *you* as *you* read this book.

Norval F. Pease

Introduction

In 1967 an important event took place related to worship among Seventh-day Adventists: the publication of *And Worship Him* by Norval Pease. Pease, a respected teacher in the Seventh-day Adventist (SDA) Church, prepared the volume while serving on the faculty of the Seventh-day Adventist Theological Seminary. It was the first of its kind for Adventists and constitutes the pioneer volume in the field. For a number of years it served as the basis for the courses on worship taught by Pease and others in the Theological Seminary and in college religion departments throughout the SDA Church. Today it can be found on the library shelves of most SDA pastors and teachers who received their advanced degrees since its publication. It ranks with the best literature produced by the SDA Church for the training of its pastors and worship leaders. It is with deep appreciation that the present writer hails this publication as foundational to all that may be said or written on the subject of worship by Seventh-day Adventists.

The present book is an attempt to build on the foundation established by Dr. Pease. Seventeen years have elapsed since the publication of *And Worship Him*. I trust that this present volume will serve in some small way to begin bridging that gap in time.

Encouragement for this project has come from many sources, from many Adventist scholars and friends over the past twelve years, many of whom have not known of their influence on my thinking. I am indebted in particular to the General Conference of Seventh-day Adventists and the Far Eastern Division for the call to serve on the faculty of the Seventh-day Adventist Theological Seminary Far East, Silang, Cavite Province, Republic of the Philippines. I am most indebted to the students who sat in my classes on worship at that warm, sunny place.

Coming, as they did, from a multicultural area of the world, from Africa, and even from northern Europe, they sparked my thinking along avenues I would not have considered otherwise. It was there that the major work on this book was done.

Specific individuals have made invaluable criticisms and suggestions. They are: Dr. Tom Blincoe, Dr. John Jones, Dr. Arnold Kurtz, and Dr. Norval Pease, who has honored me by consenting to write the foreword. Mrs. Hedwig Jemison, curator of the Ellen G. White Research Center at Andrews University, and Mrs. Gladys Benfield, president of the Seventh-day Adventist Church Musicians Guild, have provided much encouragement and support.

I am particularly grateful to the Seventh-day Adventist Church Musicians Guild for the invitation to be the keynote speaker during their annual convention held at Keene, Texas, in July 1982. There, for the first time, the basic concepts of this work were made public in the church.

While Christian worship is firmly rooted in the ancient traditions of the Word of God, that same Word calls the church of the last days to sing a new song of worship and praise to its Redeemer. This book is offered to the church with the prayer that it will help us sing that new song in meaningful and deeply spiritual celebration, as we prepare to welcome our Lord on His return.

Adventist Worship in Contemporary and Biblical Context / Part One

Adventist Worship in Perspective / 1

The Seventh-day Adventist Church has managed to avoid, to a large degree, the experimentation with new forms of worship which took place in the 1950s and 1960s in other church bodies, both Protestant and Roman Catholic. At that time the "liturgical revival," as it was called, swept through the major denominations in America and elsewhere. Change was the order of the day. Very often it was change for the sake of change. Great excitement filled theological seminaries and captured the attention of students preparing for the ministry. However, these changes in most cases left the laity mystified and confused by the frequent introduction of new hymnals and new orders of service. In one of the major Protestant denominations in the United States, for example, a new hymnal and service book was introduced to congregations twice within fifteen years. When officially adopted, these new liturgical orders became mandatory for congregations. Whether the members approved or not, whether they liked what had been done in the new hymnals or not, they were pressed to adopt and learn the new forms. A lot of grumbling and dissatisfaction was voiced by laymen and endured by pastors charged with the responsibility of making the new forms palatable and acceptable to their congregations.

It was easy to start a conversation—or an argument—among ministerial students over obscure liturgical details. I recall one debate which lasted for weeks over the type of fabric which would serve best for ministerial vestments. Another raged over the introduction of eucharistic vestments to be worn by the clergy at Holy Communion services. Another concerned the frequency of celebrating the Lord's Supper. This last elicited the comment of one seminary professor to his excited students that "you could receive communion every hour on the hour until you burp and it wouldn't do you any good!" There were other such debates too numerous and too ridiculous to mention.

It is the nature of the Christian ministry, and of the life of the church, to be excited about it all. Christian faith and life certainly ought to be exciting and challenging. However, that excitement and enthusiasm should be aroused by the message the church believes and proclaims. If the message has been lost or obscured, if the church is uncertain about the nature and content of that message, excitement and a feeling of significance are sought elsewhere. By the late '50s and '60s the world ecumenical movement, together with the directions contemporary theology was taking, had brought Christianity to a point of uncertainty as to the nature of its historic message. Even the great Lutheran churches of Europe, Scandinavia, and the United States had begun, by the time of the Lutheran World Federation meeting held in Helsinki in 1962, to lose their usual clarity and certainty regarding the Reformation doctrine of justification by faith. Large segments of once evangelistically oriented churches, such as the Methodist, Presbyterian, Baptist, and Reformed, were no longer so certain about the nature of the gospel and the purpose of the Christian church. Strong opposition prevailed against the evangelistic crusades of Billy Graham, one of the brightest lights in Protestantism since the 1950s. It was not until Mr. Graham was overwhelmingly welcomed by the grass-roots level of a world and church starved for the simple, certain, gospel message that he began to receive reluctant and scattered support for his campaigns.

The same period witnessed the phenomenal rise of Pentecostalism across denominational lines. A new excitement was generated in churches over the unusual experiences of speaking in tongues, faith healing, and exorcism. These phenomena were viewed as proof of the reality of God in the church and the world at a time when His Word was being widely doubted and consequently no longer preached with conviction and power. The situation was ripe also for a resurgence of occultism and non-Christian religions in the Western world, particularly in the United States. In addition there also appeared a number of strange pseudo-Christian movements.

The Liturgical Revival and the SDA Church

During this period the Seventh-day Adventist Church stood like a rock for historic biblical Christianity. It was not touched by these excesses, nor by the liturgical revival.

There were reasons for the fact that the Seventh-day Adventist Church avoided the experiments and consequences of the liturgical revival. First of all, it had not lost sight of the biblical message. There was no doubt among Adventist scholars, ministers, and lay members that the Bible was the inspired written Word of God, or that when its message of redemption through the blood of Jesus Christ was preached, people would hear, respond in faith, and find salvation. Furthermore, there was no doubt that God had indeed caused the emergence of this movement in the middle of the nineteenth century and prospered it, for the express purpose of not only preserving the ancient biblical heritage, but of restoring it to all of Christendom. During a time when many churches were reducing missionary budgets and personnel, there was no hesitancy among Adventists to recruit more and more missionaries and fund more missions. Seventh-day Adventists saw their mission and message as representative of a great movement near the close of human history, serving as a counter to world ecumenism and Pentecostalism. Because the Seventh-day Adventist Church was firmly committed to belief in the reliability of the Bible and was preaching the Bible's message with conviction, it was not enticed by the novelty of glossolalia or the compromising drive toward Christian unity.

The second factor contributing to the Adventist Church's stability in the face of wide-ranging theological and liturgical change was the strong influence of the writings of Ellen G. White. On virtually every page of her literary output Mrs. White pointed her readers to the Bible as the only safe guide for faith and life, and to the crucified, resurrected, and glorified Saviour as the only sure way to everlasting life. The Adventist Church's faith in the Bible as inspired by the Holy Spirit and as the means of communicating accurate and reliable information from God to man has been fortified by the literary work of Ellen G. White. Her work has served as a firm safeguard against the kind of attacks on the very source of Christian knowledge and revelation that have devastated Christianity for the past two hundred years.

Adventist believers did not have to look elsewhere for the affirmation of their faith. They did not need world ecumenism for the assurance that God was indeed calling His people into a united body. Long before the modern ecumenical movement appeared on the scene, Adventist believers were convinced that God had indeed brought their movement into being to call His people to unity. From the Bible they had, by the middle of the nineteenth century, received the message that the Lord was "gathering into one the children of God who are scattered abroad" (John 11:52). This conviction was affirmed by Ellen White.

Adventist believers did not have to turn to Pentecostalism for proof that the Lord was alive and active in His world and church. Plenty of religious excitement was available by participating in world and local evangelism, in which every member could personally share. The challenges inherent in the faithful keeping of the seventh-day Sabbath, in religious liberty issues, and in obedient Christian living served to occupy the attention of Adventist church members. Consequently the fervor of Pentecostalism made little impact.

All of these historical events in the last half of the twentieth century have influenced not only the theology, but also the worship of the church. Theology and worship are not mutually exclusive. Theology does have an effect on worship practice and forms, as we shall see in subsequent chapters.

Significance of the Liturgical Revival

Liturgical changes in the decades mentioned above were rapid and extensive, and in some cases radical as well. But the excitement of those days eventually disappeared and was replaced by other religious passions, such as the churches' concern for human rights, criticism of the Vietnam war, interest in ecology, opposition to nuclear proliferation, and even involvement in local and national as well as international political issues. Yet the impact of liturgical experimentation remained. While much of the outlandish in worship was finally abandoned upon more mature reflection, the whole experience did have a lasting influence on worship practices. The churches did not go back to a pre-1960s era in their worship.

After the dust of the liturgical revival settled and cooler heads prevailed, the churches discovered some things that Adventists had considered important for a long time. The first of these discoveries was that the important factor in worship is the people who worship and not the rituals themselves. Second, churches realized the need for variety in worship form. Worship was no longer seen as a static order of service imposed upon people whether they liked it or not. The door was now left wide open for liturgical creativity and innovation. Orders of service were no longer considered binding on congregations. Third, the gathering together of God's people in worship became more significant than the details of the service itself.

There is no doubt that the liturgical revival of the '50s and '60s was significantly related to the world ecumenical movement. Confusion about the distinctiveness of a church's message leads to experimentation with liturgical practice, it seems. Such experimentation in itself is not bad, if it is being done for the right reason. After all, if the message a church proclaims is undergoing criticism and doubt, how is it possible for the worship of the church to escape re-examination? A major consequence of this renewed focus on worship has been the interest of the churches in other liturgical traditions. Suddenly it has become fashionable to borrow across liturgical traditions, and this borrowing has been entered into with enthusiasm. With theological/doctrinal fences down, the herds have begun to mix. Liturgical cross-breeding is taking place, and the offspring are often startling. As James White points out, "When Pentecostal and Anglican traditions mingle, when Free Churchmen and Roman Catholics borrow from each other, it is obvious that we have entered a new ball game."[1]

Adventist Response to Liturgical Revival

The Seventh-day Adventist Church has something significant to say to sister churches, and to itself, concerning worship. The fundamental message of the Sabbath and the three angels of Revelation 14 is a call to worship; therefore, worship is a subject which merits attention both for our own sake and for the sake of the entire Christian community and the world.

We have a good basis from which to begin. It is a basis which seeks a scripturally inspired unity among all Christians. It is a basis which recognizes, first of all, what we hold in common with other Christians, namely, the gospel, and, second, what we have that is unique and can contribute to their, as well as our own, understanding and experience of worship.

With Lutherans we share the centrality of the Word expressed in worship in terms of preaching, as well as the sacraments of baptism and the Lord's Supper. With our Reformed friends we appreciate the role that hymnody and public prayer exercise in congregational worship. We also share with them what at times is a severe austerity in worship practices. Together with the free churches we value informality and the freedom of the congregation to determine its form of worship service. Simplicity and variety are characteristics in such a non-creedal approach to worship. The worship tradition with which Adventists have most in common is that of the Methodist Church, wherein preaching is central and extempore praying is practiced, together with much hymn singing. The Anglican and Pentecostal churches have had little influence on Adventist worship up to the present.

Since the publication of *And Worship Him* by Norval Pease in 1967 and with the influence of the Seventh-day Adventist Church Musicians Guild, there has been a slowly developing concern for worship and liturgical consciousness among Adventists. Pease's book was an understandable reaction to the excesses that were a part of the

[1]James F. White, *Christian Worship in Transition* (Nashville: Abingdon, 1976), p. 139.

Protestant liturgical revival taking place at that time. He issued a clear warning to the SDA Church concerning the danger of losing spontaneity in worship, of replacing evangelical fervor with ornamentation and liturgical embellishment. At the same time Dr. Pease insisted that the SDA Church must not rest content with worship practices that then existed. He made a strong plea for improvement and growth respecting worship and liturgics. "If we neglect beauty, order, and reverence," he said, "in an endeavor to avoid formalism and sacerdotalism, we miss a vital part of Christian worship. We need a liturgical revival, but *not* the kind that is going on in the Christian world around us."[2] We *need* a worship revival, he said! That was written in 1967, and the revival has been a long time in coming. Perhaps now we are at last beginning to see signs of such a revival in our church!

For example, in recent years there has been a growing interest among Adventists in the arts. We have learned to appreciate the relationship between worship and the human love for beauty and design. The relationship between cognition and aesthetics in the human personality is apparent, and we recognize the need to appeal to both in worship. Architecturally, more time is spent in relating what happens inside a church building to the design of the building, and we have begun to ask theological/liturgical questions *before* the design and construction phases. We are translating some of our most strongly held feelings about worship into brick and stone and lumber. We are learning to build churches that inculcate an appreciation for informality, extemporaneity, and variety. And dedicated church musicians, most of them unsalaried, have devoted much of their time, in cooperation with ministers, to the planning of worship services that touch both the mind and the heart of the worshiper. They are helping us to broaden our appreciation of the best music available, from the magnificence of the classical chorales to the heart-warming melodies of the gospel song and the spiritual.

What will we do now, as Adventists, in the light of the "new ball game" articulated by James F. White? This is certainly no time to sit in the bleachers as fascinated spectators, analyzing the game and criticizing the plays, waiting to see how the game ends. It is, rather, the time to join the game, make a bid for the mound, and start pitching. The times, the oportunity, and our biblical mandate deny us any other option.

We are on our way already but still have a way to go before our rituals catch up with our theology.

[2]Norval F. Pease, *And Worship Him* (Nashville: Southern Publishing Association, 1967), p. 44.

Discussion Questions

1. What should be the response of the SDA Church to contemporary liturgical concerns and issues?
2. On what biblical and theological bases should we participate in the liturgical dialogue?
3. What is the relationship between theology of worship, liturgical practice, art, and church architecture?

The Liturgical Mission of the Seventh-day Adventist Church / 2

A specific and distinctive liturgical mission has been given to the Seventh-day Adventist Church in a particular historical context: the ecumenical age. Our mandate is: "Fear God and give him glory, for the hour of his judgment has come; and worship him who made heaven and earth" (Rev 14:7). The first half of this biblical statement provides the historical setting: Christ has entered the second (judgment) phase of His heavenly ministry. The second half describes the major activity of the church living in that historical setting: it worships. Adventist forms of worship, therefore, must make the same connection. They must grow out of theological reflection on worship as Revelation 14 sees it: intimately related to the ministry of our Lord in heaven. Ministers and congregations that take seriously the heavenly ministry of Christ as that ministry impinges on worship will learn to think theologically and liturgically about worship.

This chapter has two goals: (1) to motivate the reader to think theologically about worship and about what happens when worship takes places; and (2) to suggest a way to meet our liturgical responsibility that is consistent with the three angels' messages of Revelation 14 and the heavenly ministry of Christ.

The ultimate goal of worship is a confrontation with God as we know Him in Christ as Seventh-day Adventists (Rev 4:11 and 5:9–10, 12–13). While worship itself constitutes the confrontation, liturgy or ritual—what we say and what we do when we worship, and how we say and do it—constitutes the articulation, the definition, the illustration of that confrontation. Thus worship and its forms become an object lesson, a living illustration and definition of what we believe. Worship serves a proclamatory, prophetic function.

Worship forms must never be viewed as ends in themselves, but as the framework for the preaching of the gospel. What we do in worship must always be interpreted by our words. What we say in worship is always more important than what we do, but what we do liturgically should be significantly related to what we say theologically. If we say the right things we ought not do the wrong things.

Worship embodies "theological declaration," says Paul Waitman Hoon. Because this is so, he goes on to say, "our conception of God and its implication for worship must be stated as clearly as possible; and the task of christian theology . . . is to impart to worship substance, purpose, and—to a considerable degree—a form consistent with belief in God deriving from christian revelation. In this sense theology may be said to exercise a generative, critical, and conservative function toward liturgy."[1] With this statement Hoon calls our attention to the critical relationship between theology and liturgy. It is a relationship that we must take very seriously if we are to fulfill our liturgical mission.

Why Do We Have a Liturgical Mission and Responsibility?

We worship today in the ecumenical age which has fostered a liturgical revival touching almost every major Protestant denomination as well as the Roman Catholic Church. Liturgiologists are careful to recognize the vital relationship between what happens in worship liturgically and its theological foundations. Norval Pease wrote: "Worship reflects the theology of the worshippers."[2] Most Christians share certain basic beliefs about God, and these shared beliefs find expression in similar forms of Christian worship. Richard Paquier has remarked: "The liturgy is a sign and indication of the communion of saints through the whole length of time and across the reaches of space. It constitutes one of the marks of the catholicity of the church."[3] By "catholicity" he means the universality, the basic unity, of Christianity. Since theology and liturgy are so intimately connected, any reevaluation of one inevitably leads to a re-examination of the other. Thus it could be wrongly concluded that as Christians unite in worship (liturgy), they also unite in belief. In this connection Paquier quotes Andre Schlemmer, a German scholar, who said, "All liturgical reform

[1]Paul Waitman Hoon, *The Integrity of Worship* (Nashville: Abingdon, 1971), p. 86.

[2]Pease, *And Worship Him*, p. 42.

[3]Richard Paquier, *Dynamics of Worship* (Philadelphia: Fortress Press, 1967), p. 51.

must lead to ecumenicity."[4] This is the objective of the World Council of Churches: uniformity in liturgical practice based on commonly held theological presuppositions.

Because we recognize the truth of these statements, and because we believe the Seventh-day Adventist Church represents the true ecumenical movement in the world, calling believers to unite in worship based on Scripture and as the Creator commands, we cannot ignore the relationship between what we believe theologically and what we do in worship liturgically. Our liturgical mission and responsibility require us to preach the biblical doctrines that explain the way to Christian unity, and also to illustrate these truths liturgically. This responsibility is inherent in the distinctive gospel message Rev 14:7 calls us to preach. The contemporary liturgical revival gives the Seventh-day Adventist Church an unprecedented opportunity to proclaim God's truth through a meaningful liturgy. We must recognize our liturgical mission—this call we are to give to all people to unite in Scriptural worship—as a "gift of the Spirit to the Church for the reedification of the body of Christ that has been torn and fragmented."[5]

Because the message entrusted to us is so important, we must be certain that our worship meaningfully expresses that message. Hoon strikingly points out that "the Reformers' insight into theological truth could not tolerate liturgical error."[6] So also our understanding of theological truth cannot overlook inaccuracy in liturgical expression. Our problem as Seventh-day Adventists is not with liturgical error; it is with liturgical ambiguity. The liturgical statement we make to the world and to ourselves each Sabbath needs to be clarified and sharpened. Precisely because the "living nerve of theology is touched in liturgy,"[7] we must take seriously the liturgical expression of our beliefs.

The Biblical Meaning of "Liturgy"

Two interrelated terms in the above discussion need clear definitions at this point. "Worship," as it is used throughout this book, refers to the Christian's total life under God, and more specifically to his/her relationship with Jesus Christ whose disciple he/she seeks to be. "Worship" also refers to the activity of the corporate body of believers gathered on the Sabbath to conduct their "liturgies," or the forms that dramatically express their faith and praise. Therefore, "worship" and

[4]Paquier, *Dynamics of Worship*, p. 51.
[5]Ibid.
[6]Hoon, *The Integrity of Worship*, p. 76.
[7]Ibid., p. 88.

"liturgy" are often used interchangeably. The term "liturgy" also can encompass the total life response of the believer to the grace and love of God revealed on Calvary and in Christ's heavenly ministry. "Liturgy" is used here more specifically, however, to refer to the order of service, whether it be on Sabbath morning or on other occasions such as baptisms, dedications, funerals, and weddings.

The term "liturgy" is a translation of the Greek New Testament terms *leitourgeo* (the verb form) and *leitourgia* (the noun form), meaning the performance of a service. In the New Testament these terms were usually linked with the term *laos* (people) in relation to services rendered to persons in the social context. It is this connotation which has resulted in referring to Christian worship as the order of *service.* Later usage, reflected in Acts 13:2 where the term is translated "worshiping," makes God the recipient of the service performed.

The Septuagint refers to the priests' ministry in the sacrificial service as *leitourgia*, but the New Testament never uses these terms in reference to the services of apostles, teachers, prophets, presbyters, bishops, or pastors. For the New Testament believers the priestly cultus had reached its end with the sacrifice and ascension of Christ, and they proclaimed in the gospel the *leitourgia* which took place on Calvary's cross and continues in Christ's heavenly ministry. The new community, the church, consists of priests who have access to God by faith in Christ, and a High Priest who is performing the *leitourgia* (ministry of service) before God on behalf of His people. Heb 8:1–2 reads:

> Now the point we are saying is this: we have such a High Priest, one who is seated at the right hand of the throne of the Majesty in heaven, a minister *[leitergos]* in the sanctuary and true tent which is set up not by man but by the Lord.

Verse six of the same chapter reads:

> But as it is Christ has obtained a ministry *[leitourgias]* which is as much more excellent than the old as the covenant He mediates is better, since it is enacted on better promises.

According to Heb 9:21–28 the work of Christ in heaven is a liturgical work. The word translated "worship" in Heb 9:21 is *leitourgias* (service), and involves purification and cleansing. This liturgical work, or ministry, of Christ is revealed as taking place just prior to His second advent and the final judgment. In this connection the following statement by the Lutheran scholar Peter Brunner is rather astounding.

> When the New Testament views the Old Testament in retrospect, it consistently adopts the linguistic usage of the Septuagint. *Leitourgia* is the sacrificial service performed in the tabernacle (Hebrews 9:21), the regular seven-day priestly service of Zacharias in the Temple in Jerusalem (Luke 1:23); *leitourgein* denotes the daily offering of sacrifice by the priest in the old covenant (Hebrews 10:11). But this *leitourgia* and *leitourgein* do not find a direct continuation among the Christians on earth. The 'continuation' of the Old Testament *leitourgia* takes place in heaven in eschatological excellence, transcendence, and absolute perfection. *Leitourgia* is the eternal sacerdotal service performed by the Crucified, exalted to the right hand of God as the liturgist of the true Heavenly Sanctuary (Hebrews 8:2, 6).[8]

The theological/liturgical error of the Christian church was the transference of the Old Testament concept of the priest to the Christian clergy rather than to Him who functions as High Priest before the very throne of God, there serving and there ministering. The church began to move in the direction of both theological and liturgical error when it failed to recognize the ministry of Christ in the heavenly sanctuary as High Priest. This is the essential truth which distinguishes the true ecumenical movement from the false. To recognize and proclaim *this* Christ and His claims on church and world is in keeping with our unique liturgical mission and responsibility as Seventh-day Adventists.

It is the church which has received and benefited from the *leitourgia* (ministry) of its ascended and glorified High Priest that will be gathered to meet Him when He comes again. That church will recognize its returning Lord and not be fooled by any false manifestation. Our liturgical mission is to proclaim His heavenly ministry and promised return by what we say and do when we worship.

However, while what we do in worship is very important in terms of proclamation and communication, we must always maintain a balanced relationship between what is happening in heaven and what happens in our churches on Sabbath morning. Highly ornate and involved liturgical worship transfers the worshiper's focus from heaven to earth, from Christ as He serves before God to pastor/liturgist as he serves before the people. In speaking of the ecumenical church, Paquier says: "Its mission is to render highest honor to God by exercising the priesthood of continual praise. It is in this high sense that we must hear the word *liturgy* and not in the narrow concept of an order of service."[9] Seventh-day Adventists ought to understand

[8]Peter Brunner, *Worship in the Name of Jesus* (St. Louis: Concordia, 1968), pp. 14, 15.

[9]Paquier, *Dynamics of Worship*, p. 56.

this better than any other Christians. Properly balanced ritual always diverts attention away from itself and toward that truth which it reenacts and proclaims.

Worship consists of what the church says and what it does when it stands before God on Sabbath morning. The combination, or the uniting of the saying and the doing, is what forms the ritual, the liturgy, of the worship service. Based on our understanding of the New Testament terms discussed above, we can define "liturgy" as the actions of a congregation responding in worship to Christ's total ministry, and the words it speaks, by means of which it illustrates and defines the content of its confrontation with God. "Liturgy" will be used in this book in reference to both the *content* and *action* of any worship service. Given its biblical meaning, the term "liturgy" can legitimately and freely be used by Seventh-day Adventist pastors and laymen. In fact, it must be understood and so used due to its vital relationship with the ministry of Christ in the heavenly sanctuary.

Implementing Our Liturgical Mission

Seventh-day Adventists know God through a grateful appreciation, not only of Christ's sacrifice on the cross, but also of His ministry in heaven. We recognize our responsibility to communicate this knowledge through our worship services. This communication *through* worship of God's call *to* worship is our "liturgical mission." The way we implement that liturgical mission—the way we conduct our worship services—must be determined by our understanding of the whole gospel message. What we do must grow out of what we believe and teach. Because it is part of communicating the gospel, what happens in worship is not a matter of indifference. It is not an incidental matter that can be left to the whim and fancy of pastors and/or presiding lay elders. It requires prayerful thought and careful planning to create a deeply meaningful service. It also requires careful education of the congregation as to the meaning of symbolic actions.

It would seem, then, that our biblical mandate requires Seventh-day Adventist worship to be distinctive. While we share many liturgical traditions with other denominations, our worship ought not be identical with theirs. The mission of the Seventh-day Adventist Church must be made audible and visible in its worship services, thereby reflecting the distinctive doctrines we hold to be essential and vital.

Norval Pease put it this way: "It is impossible to conduct a service without liturgy. . . . Our concern is that we avoid excessive and improper liturgy. By improper we mean that which is not an accurate expression of our theology."[10] Every Adventist congregation on every Sabbath is engaged in liturgical worship, whether it be of a formal or informal variety. In most cases, unless the sermon deals with doctrines unique among Adventists, the service could easily be that of a Baptist, Methodist, or Presbyterian church. But a proper Adventist liturgy is one that reflects Adventist beliefs.

There are three distinctive doctrines which ought to be illustrated liturgically in every Adventist church's worship service: the Sabbath, the heavenly ministry of Christ, and the second advent of Christ. How this is to be done leaves room for creativity and innovation on the part of pastors and lay leaders.[11]

Adventist congregations are encouraged to establish certain rules (rubrics) concerning the ordering of their worship services and activities. Ellen White wrote: "There should be rules in regard to the time, the place, and the manner of worshipping."[12] Who is to establish such rules? It would not be in harmony with our traditions if they were established by the General Conference and then imposed on congregations. Nor should ministers alone establish such rules. Ministers have a responsibility to teach congregations the relationship between theology and worship, between beliefs and rituals, and to train them to appreciate the best. To fulfill this responsibility, worship leaders must receive adequate training in harmony with Adventist theology. However, each congregation should also elect a worship committee charged with the development of orders of service that adequately reflect what the congregation believes and appreciates in worship activity. Furthermore, the liturgical life of the congregation should be under periodic review and restudy by this committee. Adventist worship should be worthy of our own great theological traditions. The responsibility for making it worthy rests with the congregation as well as the minister.

What we say and do when we worship is a collective act which defines and illustrates Adventist worship as a foretaste of the final gathering on Mount Zion and demonstrates the truly ecumenical, uniting nature of Adventism. While other churches are moving in the direction of similarity in liturgy, thus illustrating commonly held beliefs, we must respond more fully to the first angel's message of Revelation 14 and move in the direction of liturgical distinctiveness. In this way the contrast between Adventism and other churches will be more

[10]Pease, *And Worship Him*, p. 51.

[11]See Appendix A.

[12]Ellen G. White, *Testimonies for the Church*, Vol. 5 (Mountain View, Calif.: Pacific Press Publishing Association, 1948), p. 491.

apparent, and our worship will contribute to the incisiveness of the eternal gospel we are called to preach.

Discussion Questions

1. Is the premise valid that theological beliefs ought to be reflected in liturgy? If so, why? If not, why not?
2. What can be done to solve the problem of liturgical ambiguity?
3. Are the terms "liturgy" and "liturgical" legitimate for SDA dialogue on worship? Do they have an adequate biblical basis for usage?
4. What is the value of congregations' electing worship committees? Who should be members of such committees? What should be such a committee's special function?

The Focus of Adventist Worship / 3

Seventh-day Adventists of today live in the final period of mankind's history, on the very brink of God's coming kingdom. Our worship each Sabbath morning should therefore anticipate worshiping in God's presence; it should even now exhibit some of the characteristics of the worship that takes place in heaven. What is heaven's worship like? Inspiration has provided an "open door" so that God's people can catch a glimpse of the beauty and grandeur of worship in heavenly splendor. Chapters 4 and 5 of the book of Revelation provide that insight. These chapters paint a picture of heaven's worship, as it is now and as it will be for the saints in glory.

Worship in Heavenly Splendor

Revelation portrays worship in heaven as liturgical in nature, involving material, verbal, and dramatic elements. There are five verbal elements recorded, two in chapter 4 and three in chapter 5. The first is the speech of the four living creatures (Rev 4:8b), whose praise in the form of a *sanctus* (the ascription of holiness to God) never ends. The second is the words of the twenty-four elders (Rev 4:11), who respond to the *sanctus* of the four living creatures with a *doxology* (the giving of glory to God) and by casting their crowns before God's throne. The four creatures and the twenty-four elders are the proclaimers of God's Word, and in their liturgy of praise the emphasis is on God as Creator. It is His creative power and acts that lead the heavenly host to exalt His majesty.

Between chapter 4 and chapter 5, a change of emphasis occurs. In chapter 4 the focus is on God and His throne. In chapter 5 the scene and the worshipers are the same, but the focus has shifted from the

Father to the Lamb of God, Jesus Christ. In chapter 4 praise is accorded to the Father; in chapter 5 it is also accorded to the Son. Now Jesus, the overcomer (Rev 5:7), comes forward to open the *biblion*, the sealed record of human events. The act of taking the book (Rev 5:8), which demonstrates the power and authority of the Son of God to convert its prophecies into triumphant historical realities, calls forth the third verbal response: another *doxology* from the living creatures and the twenty-four elders. This doxology includes the prayers offered by all the saints on earth (Rev 5:9), the redeemed for whom Christ shed His blood and purchased redemption. It glorifies Jesus because of His victorious sacrifice on Calvary and praises His provision of redemption. He is worshiped for what He accomplished by His sacrifice on behalf of mankind. His work allows the redeemed to sing the new song which grows out of their new experience of salvation in Christ.

The fourth verbal response comes from a multitude of angels who join in the worship with a *doxology* of their own, which also acknowledges the Lamb and His sacrifice. The angels in heaven are stirred beyond measure by the effects and implications of the Lamb's great act. In the fifth verbal response the whole world joins in a mighty, united chorus of worship and praise glorifying both the Father and the Son: "To him who sits on the throne, and to the Lamb, be blessing and honor and glory and dominion forever and ever" (Rev 5:13). This fourfold utterance of praise is punctuated by loud "Amens" by the four living creatures in a choir chorus. Perhaps there is a brief silence after each ascription and then a loud "Amen" as a seal on the truth it expresses. These verbal elements of worship include the use of a loud voice, weeping, singing, and proclaiming.

This worship in heavenly splendor is also replete with material and dramatic liturgical elements. Material elements include a throne, around which the liturgical action takes place. There are white garments and golden crowns, flashes of lightning and peals of thunder, together with seven burning lamps. There are also a book, seals, harps, and golden bowls. Liturgical drama consists of sitting before the throne, falling down prostrate, the casting of crowns, and the Lamb moving forward to take the book from the right hand of the Father.

Revelation's vivid words certainly do not portray a static worship service! They describe much activity and participation on the part of heavenly worshipers, in scenes filled with dramatic action together with responsive singing and proclaiming. Such is the worship God's faithful people will enjoy and experience in heaven.

The New Song

The specifically Christian tone of worship enters Revelation's picture in chapter 5. Here is the new song in which the note of redemption and atonement appears. It rings with praise for the work and ministry of the Lord Jesus Christ on the cross and in the heavenly sanctuary. Here Christian celebration finds its focus: in the work of Jesus for our salvation. John, in vision, was privileged to witness a great heavenly celebration of that work. Its results—salvation and the worthiness of the Lamb—were celebrated with singing and rejoicing.

That worship in heavenly splendor must find its counterpart in the worship of God's people on earth. The church is a people who assemble in worship to praise the Lord for His deliverance and to anticipate His soon return. Such a worship is a recapitulation of salvation history. As it worships, the church identifies itself as the community of the redeemed and becomes part of that history. It also acts out in liturgical drama its nature as the people of God, who love and adore Him.

Christian worship is the ascription of supreme worth to God and to His Son. It celebrates the greatness of their character and their works. They, not man, are the center and focus of worship. In worship the church does not celebrate its humanity or its unity or its sanctification or its mission. It celebrates the presence of God and the Lamb. All the liturgical action in Revelation 4–5 takes place *around the throne of God.* God is glorified and His worth proclaimed before the universe. Man is not called to glorify man. Rather, God declares man's worth by His incarnation and Christ's sacrificial act of atonement. It is this fact—that God loved His people so much that He was willing to die for them—that evokes wonder and praise in worship.

The God we worship is identified as the God who created the world and all living beings. He is the God who sent His Son to pay the ransom for our sin. The Lamb is worthy to open the book in heaven because He faithfully did what He was sent to do. He won the victory over sin, death, and the devil. For this same reason He also is worthy of our worship and praise. Because of the nature of the Godhead, not every kind of worship will suffice. Not every kind of liturgical action is satisfactory. Man's position before God is indicated in Rev 5:14: "And the elders fell down and worshipped." The original Greek of that phrase means to kiss the ground, to bow down, to do obeisance. There is no glorification of man in that. Man glorifies God! Man bows before Him in the dust, taking his rightful place with other created beings, on his knees before God (Phil 2:9–11). Man, who is the beneficiary of all God is and does, acknowledges that fact in worship by which God is exalted and praised.

Worship As Celebration

Heaven's worship, as pictured in Revelation 4 and 5, is certainly celebration. When the church gathers in the presence of its Lord, its worship too should be a celebration. It should include the three activities characteristic of celebrations: remembering, thanksgiving, and dedicating. When we celebrate a wedding anniversary, for example, we remember first love, the excitement of courtship, and the beauty of the wedding ceremony. Those past memories make us thankful for the gift of the life shared with husband or wife that continues to bless us in the present, and we rededicate ourselves to that person and to the marriage for today and for the future. So it is with the church's worship celebration. The Sabbath helps the worshiping church to remember the past and God's redemptive acts in history. That remembrance, in turn, elicits thanksgiving for His past goodness, for His care. Both remembrance and thanksgiving lead to the dedication of the worshiper to God's ideals, goals, and mission. Remembering the past gives meaning to the present as the church reaches forward to the future in the celebration of worship.

These three components of celebration are included in Revelation's description of heaven's worship. The sanctus of Revelation 4:8 remembers the past and looks to the future in its song of praise to God. It recognizes God as everlasting, "who was and is and is to come." Remembrance is central in the doxology of Rev 4:11, in which the creative power and activity of God are acknowledged. Remembrance is also central in the doxology of Rev 5:9–10 in which Christ's ministry of atonement is praised (as also in Rev 5:12). Thanksgiving rings throughout the heavenly liturgy from beginning to end. It is apparent that the heavenly beings and the whole earth are rejoicing and giving thanks for the great things accomplished by the Godhead: creation and redemption. Rededication is also included in that heavenly worship. It is implied in the new song, in the heavenly beings' falling down before the throne of God, in the final doxology of Rev 5:13, and in the "Amens" and obeisant prostration of Rev 5:14 as the heavenly worshipers offer themselves to the One who both created and redeemed the world.

Celebrating the presence of God is the central characteristic of all Christian worship, just as it was central for the psalmist. "In thy presence is fullness of joy," he wrote; "in thy right hand there are pleasures forevermore" (Ps 16:11). The joy is not in the act of coming into His presence. The joy is *in* His presence, in the fact that He *is*, that He *is here*. The psalmist's greatest fear was to be separated from that presence: "Do not cast me away from thy presence, and do not take thy Holy Spirit from me. Restore to me the joy of thy salvation, and sustain me with a willing spirit" (Ps 51:11–12). To be apart from the presence of God is to be separated from the Holy Spirit, deprived of salvation and its consequent joy. "Let us come before his presence with thanksgiving; let us shout joyfully to him with psalms, for the Lord is a great God, and a great King above all gods" (Ps 95:2–3). The call to worship in His presence is this: "Repent, therefore, and return that your sins may be wiped away, in order that times of refreshing may come from the presence of the Lord" (Acts 3:19). An appropriate benediction at the close of a worship service, one that points us to the hope of experiencing His visible presence, is Jude 24–25: "Now to him who is able to keep you from stumbling, and to make you stand in the presence of his glory blameless with great joy, to the only God our Saviour through Jesus Christ our Lord, be glory, majesty, dominion and authority, before all time and now and forever. Amen."

Celebrating the victory of Christ is also central to Adventist worship. The liturgy and the doxologies of Revelation 5 praise Jesus Christ as the victorious Lamb of God, sacrificed to save sinners. The cross and the resurrection of Christ are therefore central to Adventist worship, just as they are to the church's preaching (1 Cor 15:1–8). Worship and preaching share the same focus, since it is the preaching of the gospel—the good news that Jesus died to save sinners—that makes believers who become worshipers.

These two intertwined foci of the worship celebration—the presence of God, and the victory of Christ—evoke two basic responses from the worshiper. The first, clearly expressed in the heavenly worship of Revelation 4–5, is awe—that special kind of emotion we feel when in the very presence of God. All the emotions aroused in connection with worship have their place as long as they are in harmony with awe. Awe is the worshiper's response to the awesomeness of the Almighty, to His holiness and absolute goodness. That note of awe should be heard in the manner in which we worship, in the solemnity and dignity that characterize the service. Awe is an overwhelming awareness that the most important thing in life is acceptance by God, and that we of ourselves can do nothing to make it possible or cause it to happen. It has been made possible and can happen to us because of what Jesus did on Calvary, in His resurrection and ascension, and in His ministry in heaven.

These acts of Christ inspire the worshiper's second response: faith in the God who would make such a sacrifice for sinners. Worship assumes faith. One who does not believe will hardly worship. It is possible to "go to church" yet never worship. True worship is an expression of faith. To know God in Christ is to love Him, and to love Him is to worship Him. We are rebels at heart and it is only the death and victory of Christ that makes possible the changing of a rebel into a reborn saint. What happened in Christ happened for us, to make that transformation possible and to restore us to the presence of God.

The two foci of Christian worship celebrations are thus inseparably related. We celebrate coming into God's presence, which is made possible by the victory of Christ. In fact, the basic message of the New Testament is that God's presence is to be found in His Son (Matt 1:23, John 1:1–5). The presence of God in His Son has taken the place of His presence in the Temple. He has come to our world and lived our kind of life and suffered our kind of temptation and been victorious, not simply as an example of the possibility of holiness, but as the vicarious and substitutionary Saviour.

On Calvary we come to the core of revelation and the incarnation. Here God's resolution of man's problem of guilt and estrangement is centered. The entire biblical record focuses on Calvary. The whole story of the life of Christ centers around that event. The cross is at the core of the life and the proclamation of the Christian community. It is the focus of the Sabbath and is central to the church's worship. It is the essence of the church's hope, for without atonement there would be no second advent and no everlasting life. In fact, without the atonement there would be no church and no worship. The realization of God's incomparable act on Calvary gives grateful voice to the sanctus and the doxology and the new song of worship in heavenly splendor.

Worship is a retelling of the gospel story, a dramatization liturgically, in baptism, footwashing, and holy communion, of the atoning sacrifice of Christ. We remember the awesome truth of that sacrifice with wonder, dread, fascination, and utter dependency. We are deeply and humbly thankful for what God has done. The truth of it, the reality of it, the power of it, moves the church and its people to weekly dedication. Worship, through this remembrance, thanksgiving, and dedication, becomes the impetus for our evangelism and mission, just as the angels that participate in heavenly worship then fly in midheaven with a message to proclaim to every nation on earth.

That proclamation includes an invitation to the church of the last days, and to the whole world, to join in the singing of the new song.

It is a song of remembrance, of faith, and of hope. It is a new song sung by a new people in a new day, in a new way, and, finally, on a new earth. It is a song about the Lamb that was slain, about His creative power, His redemptive love, His daily care from heaven, and His glorious return. To worship is to sing it, and to sing it is to worship. To sing it together now is to rehearse for that great day when His people will join the heavenly hosts in everlasting praise of the Father and the Son, when the curtain is raised on the final act in the drama of history.

Discussion Questions

1. What can be done to assist SDA worshipers to move from a passive to a more active participation in worship?
2. What can be done to help SDA church members appreciate the liturgical symbolism of worship?
3. What can be done to help SDA church members think of, and experience, worship as celebration?

Adventist Worship in Theological Context / *Part Two*

Worship and the Sabbath / 4

The Sabbath was a gift from God to all of His people to establish and perpetuate true worship through time and eternity. This gift was not just for a select few, but for all mankind at all times. It is not possible for a Seventh-day Adventist to think about worship or to participate in worship without reference to the Sabbath and its meaning. As one of the three major biblical doctrines which identify Adventists, the Sabbath should be liturgically dramatized and illustrated in every worship service. It is one of the constants of the order of service.[1] As a worshiping Seventh-day Adventist, I want to share with my reader what the Sabbath has come to mean to me and to my worship, in terms of my attitude toward time, toward work, toward human limitations, and toward rest.

Attitudes Toward Time

I used to speak of "killing" time. The Sabbath should help to purge such expressions from our use of language! Time is one of God's greatest gifts to a human being. In fact, it is His fundamental gift: the gift of life itself. Almost as bad as killing time is wasting such a precious and rare commodity. Time belongs to God, not to us. We have no control over when and where and to whom we are born, or when and where and under what circumstances we will die. Time and life are both gifts of God and they must be enjoyed and used accordingly.

Today people think of God as present in space, in things, in churches, in nature, rather than in events and history. Pantheism, for

[1]Constants are those parts of the order of service which do not change in emphasis from week to week. Variables are those parts whose content and/or emphasis does change from week to week. See chapter 8.

example, is a religion of space. It thinks of God as being infinite spatially—in the sense of the expansiveness of the universe—rather than as an eternal and everlasting Being who is active in the world as well as above the world. But Christianity is a religion of time before space. In the beginning of earth's history God did not consecrate a place for His dwelling. Rather, He consecrated a period of time in which His creatures were to meet Him in fellowship and communion. Thus He made man a steward of time as well as of life and of tangible created things.

We know what to do with space, the material part of God's creation. We fill it with all manner of things, some beautiful and many ugly. We don't know what to do with time, so we "waste" time, "pass" time, and "kill" time. But the Sabbath reminds us of the sacredness of all time and of that day in particular. It serves, as Abraham Heschel points out, to help us "face sacred moments."[2] The Sabbath reminds us that we are stewards of God's gift of time as well as of His material gifts. It reminds us to use the gift of time to the glory of God and the edification and well-being of mankind.

Both space and time are to be consecrated by the use to which they are put. Each of us has been granted a small share of the vastness of eternity, a small part of history in which to live and experience the joys and sorrows of existence, and in which to work for God. We often think of time in terms of enjoyment and personal use, but we must also think of it in terms of responsibility and accountability. Time is as sacred as life itself. As we maintain the holiness of time, we maintain the holiness of life. For Sabbathkeepers this is particularly true. To give lip service to the seventh-day Sabbath, the evidence of God's claim on our time, and to spend time in any unholy activity on the Sabbath or any other day, is to desecrate the whole concept and purpose of the holiness of time.

We creatures, being sinners in a fallen world, desecrate everything that is holy. The Sabbath is no exception. As with everything man touches, the Sabbath today is desecrated and used for all manner of activities out of harmony with the will of God and the benefit of mankind. And man's misuse of time is not limited to the Sabbath. Just as he corrupts life, man corrupts all time. Often he turns time into a horror and uses it to exploit, persecute, and destroy. Such use of time reflects his rejection of God and denial of the holiness of life. The apostle Paul expressed man's misuse of God's gifts like this: "They exchange the truth about God for a lie; they worship and serve what God has

[2]Abraham Heschel, *The Sabbath* (New York: Farrar, Straus, and Young, 1951), p. 6.

created instead of the Creator himself, who is to be praised forever" (Rom 1:25, TEV).

Time is given to man to believe, to worship, and to serve God and humanity—to obey the will and commands of God as a joyful response of faith. This has been true since time began. Before the fall God revealed His will to Adam, saying, "From any tree of the garden you may eat freely; but from the tree of the knowledge of good and evil you shall not eat, for in the day that you eat of it you shall surely die" (Gen 2:16–17). Here God gave Adam both a promise and a warning. This word established a relationship between God and man. Man was called upon to behave in a certain way, to use his time to live in an obedient relationship to God.

Whenever God gives His Word to man as promise and warning, the community of the faithful—those who cherish His promise and heed His warning—is established. These believers respond to Him with faith in the validity of His word and also with willing obedience to His principles and ideals, and these concrete acts of obedience give visible expression to the invisible relationship between the community and God. Worship, particularly corporate worship during the Sabbath time God has set aside for just that purpose, is one of these concrete acts that make faith visible. In worship the believer observes the sacredness of Sabbath time (and all time), hears the Word again, renews his vow of faith and commitment, and chooses to live obediently in time and space. This, then, is the proper use of Sabbath time: to hear, learn, and do the word of God. Observing the Sabbath in this way should lead to the right use of all time.

The Sabbath reminds us of creation, when God gave us the time we now have, and redemption, in which He gives us all eternity. The celebration of creation and redemption, to which the Sabbath points, is the focus of worship for the church of the last days. That's what the worshiping church is called to "remember" when it gathers on Sabbath morning. In worship the church reminds itself, in speech and action, of the creative power of God and of His great love which has made redemption possible. It remembers its creaturely dependence upon Him for the gift of life, for the sustenance of life, and for the gift of salvation in Christ.

The perpetual nature of the Sabbath in time and eternity reminds us of the faithfulness of God over against our unfaithfulness. The Sabbath comes faithfully every seventh day, whether we acknowledge it or not, just as Jesus would have died on the cross though no one would believe. God is faithful though we are unfaithful. He can be depended upon. He always does what He says He will do. His word becomes deed. He keeps His promises.

God's faithfulness has implications for our life of faith as well. Just as His love for man was acted out in historic events, so our faith in God must be acted out in loving service. Faith can only be expressed by specific acts in time and space. Worship provides one opportunity to affirm our faith by our actions. As we worship we enter into the holiness of sacred time and participate in its blessings; we act out in liturgical drama the events of holy history which are to be remembered. Remembering keeps them ever fresh, ever new, ever alive in our minds and before our eyes. Renewed by this remembrance of God's great gifts, we leave the worship service to live our faith in the time God gives us for the days to come.

Attitudes Toward Work

Human life on this earth began with God in worship, and it is to end with God in worship. In thus encompassing our lives with His presence, God claims the whole of our lives—everything that happens between beginning and ending—as his own. The Sabbath makes a similar claim. Two Sabbaths enfold each week, like two hands holding something good. What happens between those Sabbaths is just as much God's as is the Sabbath itself. Our worship is not confined to the Sabbath alone. The whole of life is to be lived in terms of worship.

The Sabbath commandment itself embodies this wholeness. It stands at the center of the Ten Commandments, and is the point of transition from our relationship to God to our relationship to man. The consequence of keeping the first three commandments—those defining our relationship to God—is to worship God on the special day He has set aside for that purpose. The worship of God, in turn, results in the kind of human relationships the rest of the commandments demand. A right relationship to God, expressed and nurtured in worship each Sabbath, forms the basis for all our working relationships with others during the week.

Sabbath indicates that God claims, not merely a special time for the special activity of worship, but the whole of time. God has given us one day out of seven for fellowship with Him and six days out of seven for work in the world. On one day believers are to worship God; on six days they are to work and serve mankind.

Often the way in which we observe the Sabbath gives the idea that it is work which gives Sabbath its significance. We view the Sabbath as the end of our work. "Thank God the Sabbath has come!" we often hear. But it is not work which makes the Sabbath significant. It is the Sabbath which makes work significant. Sabbath time forms the boundary around work time—it encompasses it, encloses it, encapsulates it—as though work time was held in the two hands of God. "Six days you shall labor and do all your work" is as much a command of God as "remember the Sabbath day to keep it holy." This command sanctifies labor as an act of faith and obedience to God—truly an act of worship. So worship involves more than what we do in church on the Sabbath. It involves what we do in the world on the other six days. On the Sabbath our service to God through our work is interrupted for the special activity of worship, study, and renewal of fellowship with God, so that we can work as faithful servants of God in the world for the rest of the week.

Working days and Sabbath days are to be understood in relation to each other. We cannot rightly understand the sanctity of labor if we do not first understand the sanctity of the Sabbath. We cannot see our work and responsibility in the world, cannot undertake our work in freedom and appreciation and eagerness, except in relation to its boundary. We must view all of time from the perspective of the Sabbath. It puts all of life into the proper perspective and relationship. The Sabbath prepares us to face our work with eagerness and renewed zeal and dedication as unto the Lord.

While we need to think of the Sabbath as rest from work, we also need to think of it in relation to work. The Sabbath, and all that it signifies and contains, makes it possible for a person to take up his position *in* the world and not separated from it. In worship each Sabbath we answer God's call, and we are edified and sustained to answer His further call to "go into all the world." We seek, not escape from the world, but that which alone can prepare us for life and work in the world: fellowship with the Father, who is the source of strength and inspiration. On the Sabbath God's people are equipped by the evangel (the gospel) so they can live evangelistically for the next six days. God calls us to Himself in worship so He can send us into the world in work and service.

There is a divine relationship between Sabbath and work. To separate them is dangerous to a proper understanding of life under God. If we separate them, all we can hope for is to live with an unrelieved and guilty conscience, feeling condemned for doing "secular work" rather than "God's work." But God wants us to live in freedom, without the condemnation of conscience. So he commands both labor and rest, both work and worship. Each enhances the other and makes the other meaningful and blessed. It is only when vocation is fulfilled in responsibility that the conscience can be free within the parameters of life as God has established it.

Labor for the Sabbatarian Adventist needs to be defined, not in the exclusive terms of the Calvinist work ethic, but in terms of the radical demands in the 1980s and 1990s for the stewardship of natural resources and the environment. Only when seen in relation to rest can labor involve human responsibility *for* the earth instead of exploitation *of* the earth. Calvin ignored God's call for rest, both for man and creation, and the age of anxiety was born. His theology not only prepared man for the machines that would enslave him and pollute his world, but also for the diseases peculiar to the technological age: stress, anxiety, hypertension, industrial poisoning, etc. Urged on by Calvin and others, and to the glory of God, the man of modern times marched into the factories and mine pits that in just 200 years would waste the earth and bring civilization to the brink of extinction. The wealth produced would end up ultimately threatening life rather than enhancing it. The age of that kind of work is over. The age of rest has begun. It will be interesting to see what evangelical Christianity does now with the biblical concept of Sabbath rest.

Attitude Toward Human Limitations

The Sabbath, when viewed as we have described above, urges us into action, into using our time to live our faith, into working in society as a part of our worship of God. But the Sabbath also calls a halt to our action and is thus a vivid reminder of human limitation. While God commands us to work, He also, through the gift of the Sabbath, limits our work. We do not have the kind of power and strength God Himself has. We are creatures of limitations, and the Sabbath reminds us of that fact each week. Strange that we should need a frequent reminder of those limitations! But sin so perverted our perception of ourselves that God, in divine foresight, established the Sabbath not only as an opportunity for special fellowship with Him, but also as a perpetual reminder that we are but creatures and totally dependent on Him.

We have created nothing. We do not owe our existence to ourselves. Our ability and strength to work are gifts of God. Our future and our present success do not lie in our own power. What we are required to do is place ourselves completely at God's disposal. This the Sabbath command enjoins. It points to God as the source of all power and grace, without which we could not exist.

The Sabbath prohibits satisfaction with our own accomplishments. It prohibits faith in our own plans, wishes, and abilities. It prohibits trust in our own work. Work we must, but we are not to put our trust in it. Work is holy activity, but it is not our only activity. There is a time to do and a time to be; a time to work hard and a time to catch the breath; a time to use God-given strength and a time to accept human limitations.

Furthermore, the Sabbath reminds us of our ultimate limitation: death. Just as creation ended and God finished His work, so our life on earth will end and our course be finished. We are not only limited in our abilities; our very existence is limited. The interruption of our work by the Sabbath, whether we will or not, is a vivid reminder that death will interrupt our lives, whether we will or not. While the Sabbath tells us of God's everlasting power and perpetuity, it tells us also of our powerlessness and transitoriness, of our inability to change our situation or to help ourselves out of it. The New Testament tells us that Jesus rested in His tomb over the Sabbath. Perhaps that means more than an observance of the Sabbath day. Perhaps it too is a reminder of the weakness of humanity and of death, that the grave awaits all, that we are dust and shall return to dust.

But the Sabbath symbolizes much more than human limitation. It is primarily a symbol of life. Jesus healed on the Sabbath day. Following His crucifixion He rested in the tomb on the Sabbath day. It is a day that leads to life, not death. While death is at the end of life as we know it, death is not *the* end. On the other side of death is the resurrection! As Jesus passed through the Sabbath to resurrection, so we pass through our Sabbaths on the way to glory, by faith looking beyond death to resurrection and everlasting rest and eternal Sabbathkeeping. Sabbath is a symbol of glory!

For worshiping men and women the Sabbath is a sign of God's great ability and their own great inability. It is a form of renunciation: renunciation of human arrogance and pride; renunciation of things in favor of eternal values; renunciation of the false sense of security and self-sufficiency which often comes about by mankind's energetic and successful work. It is a call to remember human frailty. When a person is brought to a standstill before the Creator each Sabbath in worship, he becomes conscious of God's sovereignty and of his own dependent nature. All false sense of personal security vanishes before the truth. Past and future, history and eternity, meet in the seventh-day Sabbath.

Worship each Sabbath offers a weekly new beginning, a fresh start, an anticipation of resurrection and eternal life with God. It is when we participate in the preservation of the meaning of God's love and its historical manifestation that we can maintain the reality of our human condition. The Sabbath worship service offers the weekly chance to remember our dependence, which we so often forget, and to renew our relationship with the Creator so as to live freely as His creatures. Here, in worship, we accept our limitations and turn to the Lord of the Sabbath for the grace we need to live as productive servants.

Attitude Toward Rest

Because of the hectic pace of our busy twentieth-century lives, we often think of the Sabbath primarily in terms of rest, as a day to recover from our exhaustion after a week of overwork. But the Sabbath was not intended to be merely a respite from the wearying work of each week. It was created as a time for fellowship of man with God, a time for preparation for the week to come rather than for recovery from the week just past. Sabbath as "rest *from*" is a secondary concept that came into the picture after man's fall into sin. Even at Sinai rest did not dominate the meaning of the Sabbath. "Six days you shall labor and do all your work," God said; no direct mention was made of rest. The emphasis, rather, was on the worship of the Creator by the creature. A strong emphasis on Sabbath rest did not appear until Ex 31:13–17: "On the seventh day there is a Sabbath of complete rest, holy to the Lord . . . so the sons of Israel shall observe the Sabbath and celebrate the Sabbath throughout their generations as a perpetual covenant."

Before the fall the Sabbath declared the glory of God as Creator. It symbolized in time a relationship of love and freedom between God and man. It was God's offer of unmerited, unlimited, everlasting (perpetual) grace and fellowship. It was preparation for life as God's people on earth.

After the fall of man the Sabbath declared the glory of God as Redeemer and Sanctifier. The fellowship which man had known without sin was now offered in love and grace because of sin. Before the fall man enjoyed the Sabbath in unblemished fellowship with God; after the fall his fellowship with God took place in terms of restoration. Sabbath observance made possible the ministry of the means of grace in order to free man from bondage to sin. The Sabbath was an opportunity, not only for the worshiper to exercise memory, but for God to exercise restorative grace and power in the life of the worshiper. Ex 31:13 indicates that the keeping of the Sabbath included the acceptance of God's sanctifying activity. To profane the Sabbath was to deny or reject His sanctifying influence. Such rejection led to death—above all, spiritual death. True Sabbath rest consists of entering the faith relationship with Jesus the High Priest (Hebrews 4).

"Let us therefore draw near with confidence to the throne of grace, that we may receive mercy and may find grace to help in time of need" (Heb 3:16). This is a summary of what ought to happen in worship: the sinner confidently comes into the presence of God in recognition and grateful acceptance of His grace, and in order to find help for living successfully in this world. "The Sabbath was made for man, and not man for the Sabbath. Consequently, the Son of Man is Lord even of the Sabbath," said Jesus (Mark 2:27–28). The great principle He enunciated here is that the Sabbath was always intended for man as a blessing. It was meant to be a benefit, not a burden.

After the fall the Old Testament instruction about the Sabbath included physical rest from work and labor, and that is important because we need physical rest. All week long we work and use up reserves of physical energy which must be restored. This is especially true in the modern world of the twentieth century when life is lived much faster than at any other time. None of us would want to go back to the good old days. We like today's advantages of swift travel, the acquisition of good books, the wider dissemination of news, the opportunities for education, and the broadening of views. Yet all of this tires us out rapidly. We need rest. We need time to take stock, to take the long look at ourselves, at our hopes and dreams and accomplishments and failures. We need an opportunity to get a perspective on our lives. This is what the Sabbath should provide. But I fear that all the Sabbath means to many of us is a time to recover from exhaustion and fatigue.

However, recovery was not the primary intention of the Sabbath. Rest means more than recovery from fatigue. It means support. It means leaning upon or resting upon something or someone. To rest means to rest *upon* and not just *from*. We are not talking about mere physical exhaustion. We are talking about spiritual weariness: the weariness that comes when a person's life is disoriented, without plan or purpose, without goals or focus, with no clear objectives and many conflicting interests. A person who has no internal peace is one who has no eternal peace, one in whose life many things are working against each other. In such a life there is conflict between a right intuition and a wrong philosophy, which brings about guilt.

If this is the kind of exhaustion we are talking about, rest is not found merely by refraining from physical labor. To refrain from work provides the opportunity to rest upon and in the Lord, to find respite from spiritual weariness and time for the quest for meaning, to allow that which is holy to come into our lives. This is rest in the sense of peace of mind and soul, of spiritual wholeness. It is the kind of rest the Bible portrays. "For thus the Lord God, the Holy One of Israel, has said: 'In repentance and rest you shall be saved, in quietness and trust is your strength'" (Isa 30:15). "Rest in the Lord and wait patiently for Him; fret not yourself because of him who prospers in the way, because of the man who carries out wicked schemes. Cease from anger and forsake wrath: fret not yourself, it leads only to evil doing. For evil doers will be cut off, but those who wait for the Lord, they will inherit the land" (Ps 37:7–9). Jesus said, "Come to me, all who are weary and heavy laden, and I will give you rest. Take my yoke upon you, and learn from me, for I am gentle and humble in heart; and you shall find rest for your souls" (Matt 11:28–29).

Apart from this kind of rest there is no Sabbath rest. As Lord of the Sabbath, Jesus must be the center of our lives. The Sabbath gets its meaning for the Christian from Christ. His rest brings order out of confusion and offers an escape from meaninglessness. Meaning can only be found in God, in His direction and fellowship, as we learn to lean on Him, depend on Him, rest upon and in Him. It is this rest that gives meaning to work. Such rest puts everything in order in life and gives purpose to an otherwise purposeless existence. Thus the Sabbath has a redemptive meaning. It is restorative. To be redeemed does not mean only that we go to heaven eventually. It means that God has put our present lives in order. This is rest as opposed to unrest.[4]

When God rested on the seventh day from His work, it was not because He was exhausted. It was because He was establishing the opportunity for man and woman to seek and maintain a sustaining relationship with the source of all power and strength. Sabbath is for man, for the relationship between God and man.

Heb 4:1 speaks of "entering His rest." Man's rest ends and he must go back to work, but God's rest is everlasting rest. His rest, which we are to enter, began at creation and will never end. It is an everlasting rest. Heb 3:19 tells us of the only thing that will keep us from entering His everlasting rest: "And so we see that they were not able to enter because of unbelief." "Therefore, let us fear lest, while a promise remains of entering his rest, any one of you should seem to come short of it. For indeed we have had good news preached to us, just as they did also; but the word they heard did not profit them, because it was not united by faith in those who heard. For we who have believed enter that rest" (Heb 4:1–4). Rest by faith in Christ comes by way of pardon and sonship. So by faith in the present we are able to enter into the timeless Sabbath rest of God, which means to rest upon Him in complete creaturely dependence and need. Here limited man's need for a limitless God is fulfilled!

So God's rest is actually His redemptive activity, which has been uninterrupted and will continue uninterrupted until Jesus comes again. Christ is the supreme manifestation of that rest. The weekly Sabbath is forgetful man's gracious reminder of his rest in Christ. The

[4]Samuele Bacchiocchi, *Divine Rest for Human Restlessness* (published by author, 1980), pp. 189–190.

nature of Sabbath rest is to cease from work, which means to stop our own doing and let the Lord do the doing (see Heb 3:19, 4:2, 3, 11). We are to be "diligent to enter that rest" (Heb 4:11) by the exercise of faith rather than unbelief. It is not a transitory rest, incomplete, unsatisfying, and powerless. It is an everlasting rest which is not ineffective. It provides what it promises: rest for the sin-sick, sin-weary soul and mind. In contrast to our human limitations, it meets every need. So we are able to draw near to God in confident faith to receive the gifts of grace needed for successful living and service.

Worship for the Christian centers in redemption, and redemption centers in Christ. We do not worship because of the Sabbath. We worship on the Sabbath because of what Christ has done, and is doing, for us redemptively. It is His act of redemption that gives meaning to the seventh-day Sabbath. Redemption is the fulfillment of the Sabbath's meaning.

The first Sabbath celebrated by Adam was not kept in terms of atonement.[5] There was peace between God and man and no sacrifice was required. In Adam's worship before the fall there were no restrictions or penalties. In pristine worship he did not know any tension between righteousness and rebellion, between faith and repentance. Prior to the fall his relationship with God was spontaneous and free. He loved God with a completeness and freedom of expression that we can only glimpse from time to time. This was his daily experience, the context in which he lived and worshiped.

In contrast to Adam's experience, our worship is regulated by sin on the one hand and grace on the other. Our worship, with its liturgical symbols, points to the blood of Calvary, by which we have been reconciled to God. It is no accident of history nor perversion of the faith that most Christian churches display the symbol of the cross. The cross of Christ represents our faith, our hope, our need and its fulfillment, our sin and God's loving grace. Whereas Adam's pre-fall worship reflected his created likeness to God, ours must reflect our *restored* likeness to God. Such is the significance of worship in the present time. On the Sabbath we remember—we look back to the revelatory acts of God which make salvation possible. We also experience this salvation now as faith and hope, and we rest in Christ. As we yield in faith to Christ's claim on our lives, what could possibly be a better use of God's gift of time than, in work and worship, to praise both Creator and Redeemer with the new song of redemption and everlasting rest.

[5]See Brunner, *Worship in the Name of Jesus*, pp. 40–44.

Discussion Questions

1. Granted that the Sabbath, in view of its regularity and perpetuity, reminds us of and proclaims the faithfulness of God, what implications does this have with respect to the faithfulness of His people in corporate worship?
2. How should we understand and practice the relationship between worship and work, between the Sabbath and the other six days?
3. Do Sabbath and worship have anything to say in regard to a Christian work ethic?
4. Is there any experiential relationship between the Sabbath and Rom 6:1–14?

Worship and the Heavenly Ministry of Christ / 5

For many Christian groups, worship centers on something that happened in the past: the life, death, and resurrection of Christ. Seventh-day Adventist worship centers not only on past events, but also on something that is happening in the present, something that will also have a determinative influence on the future. Thus all three time dimensions of human existence—past, present, and future—are involved in worship. When Adventists gather for worship they are by faith connected, not simply with past historical events, but also with the present ministry of the Lord in the heavenly sanctuary.

This worship has its focus in heaven, while anticipating the effects of heavenly events on human experience. Objective truth must always be subjectively experienced or it is not real for the individual. In worship the heavenly events, which occur independently of the worshiper, make contact with his life. In this chapter we will discuss worship in terms of the heavenly with respect to its issue and focus, and in terms of the human with respect to the possibility of a confident approach to God and the cleansed conscience that results.

The Issue

The first three commandments make it clear that God alone is to be worshiped, and that this worship is expressed in acts of obedience. This issue was introduced in the very beginning of history, following the fall into sin. It was the fundamental issue throughout Israel's history, and it is really the issuc in the closing period of time. It is both a theological and an existential issue, both cosmic and personal. In fact, it is brought to a head in the final period of time, precisely because man's opportunity is slipping by rapidly. We believe we are in the time depicted in Revelation 13–14 and that God through His church is extending a clear call to the entire world to worship Him in faith and obedience. The last use of the word "worship" in the Bible is in Rev 22:9, where, after John the Revelator fell down at the feet of an angel who had spoken to him, the angel said, "Worship God." This is really the sum and substance of it all.

Why has this particular call been made with such urgency and emphasis? Has there been some historical event that has made God respond in the dramatic manner represented by the three angels "flying" from the heavenly sanctuary and speaking with a "loud voice"? Yes, there has, and it is described in chapter 13 of Revelation. A threatening situation has developed in the world. A false message is being preached far and wide. People are won to worship a false god by means of this apparently authoritative and impressive proclamation. The message is a blasphemous one, opposed to the true God. It seems about to eliminate faith in the true God, thereby discrediting Him before the whole world. Those who refuse to acknowledge the authority and power of the apostate religious system proclaiming this message are marked for destruction.

Revelation here pictures a false god winning people to worship him by means of a false message preached by a false church to the whole world. The world and the Christian church are in grave danger. Heaven's response is immediate and powerful: a clear message comes from the throne of God. The issue is joined, and a unique church, a remnant, is called into being to confront the false gospel with the true gospel. False preaching and false worship are challenged—challenged by the same message the apostle Paul preached on Mars Hill, calling people to put away all false gods and worship the true God alone.

This critical situation does not cause weeping and wailing among the heavenly hosts. Instead a liturgy of praise is heard. The angelic choir sings the doxology of the "new song." Heaven sees the situation as a divine opportunity and as a prelude to the return of the Lord to earth. Jesus stands in the midst of the symbolic 144,000 and exercises His sovereign care over His world and His people.

The new and emerging church preaches the everlasting gospel, sounding a clarion call to fear God, to give Him glory, and to worship Him alone. The time has come to make a clear choice! According to the first angel of Revelation 14, therefore, worship is the great cosmic and personal issue of earth's final hour. Man and the universe are to give almighty God the allegiance due His name.

The third angel of Revelation 14 underscores the message of the first angel with a strong note of warning that it is not possible to worship the true God truly without obedience. Jesus put it like this:

> Why do you call me, Lord, Lord, and yet do not do what I tell you? Anyone who comes to me and listens to my words and obeys them—I will show you what he is like. He is like a man who, in building his house, dug deep and laid the foundation on rock. The river overflowed and hit that house but could not shake it because it was well built. But anyone who hears my words and does not obey them is like a man who built his house without laying a foundation; when the flood hit that house it fell at once—and what a terrible crash that was! (Luke 6:46–49, TEV).

The faithful worshipers of God are described in Rev 14:12: "This calls for endurance on the part of God's people, those who obey God's commandments and are faithful to Jesus" (TEV). Faith and obedience are inseparably linked. One who truly worships God will trust in Jesus and obey His word, and those who trust and obey will worship.

This is why attention is centered on the heavenly sanctuary in these closing days of history. That is where the final questions and issues about the lives of God's people and His right to obedient worship are to be resolved. The whole purpose of Christ's ministry on earth and in heaven is to bring people to praise God in worshipful living. In our worship we enter the heavenly sanctuary by faith and are able to see the world, the purpose for the church, the ministry of our Lord, and our own lives from God's all-encompassing perspective and not just from our own limited, self-centered, and narrow point of view.

The Focus

The life of the Seventh-day Adventist Christian has a concrete focal point that controls and directs and defines his entire existence. This focal point is the ministry of Christ, which rests on the events of Calvary but which has now shifted to the heavenly sanctuary. Adventist worship is focused on the present activity of our Lord, who has died for us and now lives for us, making intercession before the throne of God. When Seventh-day Adventists assemble for worship they not only exercise historical memory and "remember" past events in the history of God's grace, but their faith actively reaches into the realms of heaven itself today. Such faith follows Jesus from the cross to the crown, from the thorns on His brow to the throne of God.

In worship Adventists share in the presently occurring events in heaven where history is being made now that will have an everlasting effect on the final events on earth. The Bible indicates that earth and heaven are wedded (Matthew 24; Revelation 4–5, 8–22). What happens on earth affects heaven, and what happens in heaven affects events on earth. The books of Revelation and Hebrews (Heb 4:14–16, 8–10) make that relationship unmistakably clear. Christ's words to His disciples during His earthly appearances between His resurrection and ascension indicate a relationship between the work He was going to heaven to do and the work they were given to do on earth. This connection, this relationship, intensifies as earth's history draws to a close. Heaven stands ready to set in motion the final events on this planet, and the church on earth urgently proclaims God's last message to the human race.

As eschatological historical events on earth unfold in response to the ministry of Christ in heaven, the future of the church and of all mankind is determined and fulfilled. It is not the activity of the church on earth that determines such future eschatological events, though it does have an effect on them. The determination of all such future events is made in heaven, but the faithfulness or unfaithfulness of the church in its evangelistic and serving mission will have an effect on those events. The church has been established to participate in the finishing of God's work in the world and in that sense it affects the events of the future now being determined and shaped in heaven. It is as the worshiping church that it will have this effect.

Such a close and vital relationship between events in heaven and events on earth ought to arouse our intense interest in what is happening in heaven as the ministry of our Lord there impinges on our worship life and experience. Heb 1:2 tells us that in the last days God is speaking to His people and His world through His Son. That has specific reference to His ministry in heaven. It is of the resurrected and ascended Christ that Hebrews speaks. From heaven He radiates God's glory, represents God's nature, and sustains all things while seated at the right hand of God (Heb 1:3). He is greater than the angels (chapter 2), greater than Moses (chapter 3), and identified as High Priest (Heb 2:17; 3:1; 4:14–15). After describing the role of the Old Testament high priest the writer says: "Now the main point in what has been said is this: we have such a High Priest who has taken His seat at the right hand of the throne of the majesty in the heavens, a minister in the sanctuary, and in the true tabernacle, which the Lord pitched, not man" (Heb 8:1–2). It is because we have such a High Priest ministering in heaven that the writer says further: "Let us draw near with confidence to the throne of grace" (Heb 4:16). This is obviously a reference to the worship of God's people. Heb 8:2 says Christ is a "minister in the sanctuary," and Heb 8:6 says "he has obtained a more excellent ministry." In Hebrews the term "liturgy" is introduced as Christ is spoken of as the heavenly liturgist or minister. The term helps us understand the relationship between His heavenly ministry and the worship of the church in the time of the end.

Originally this term was used in the areas of political and constitutional law. It was, as we have noted, a secular term used in reference to services performed on behalf of individuals in the social context. The German translation is *volkswerk* or *volksdienst,* work done for the people, or service done for the people. The *Apology of the Augsburg Confession* contains the following statement by Philip Melanchthon:

> It does not really mean a sacrifice but a public service. . . . Thus the term "liturgy" squares well with the ministry. It is an old word, ordinarily used in public law. To the Greeks it meant "public duties" like the taxes collected for equipping a fleet. . . . In 2 Cor 9:12 Paul uses this word for a collection. Taking this collection not only supplies what the saints need but also causes many to thank God more abundantly. In Phil 2:25 he calls Epaphroditus a "minister to my needs" which surely does not mean a sacrifice. But further proofs are unnecessary since anyone who reads Greek authors can find examples everywhere of their use of "liturgy" to mean public duties or ministrations. Because of the diphthong, philologists do not derive it from *lite,* which means prayers, but from *leita,* which means public goods; thus the verb means to care for or to administer public goods.[1]

The point is that in its original and biblical usage the term referred to a service done *for* the people and not by the people. This is highly important as we study its usage with respect to the ministry of Christ in heaven. In the Old Testament *leitourgia* the sacrificial service was performed by the priest in the tabernacle as he "sprinkled both the tabernacle and all the vessels of the ministry *(leitourgias)* with the blood" (Heb 9:21). It was the daily offering of a sacrifice by the priest in the old covenant: "And every priest stands daily ministering *(leitourgein)* and offering time after time the same sacrifice, which can never take away sins" (Heb 10:11). It was done *for* the people. But now in Christ a significant change takes place. This service does not continue among believers on earth. It continues in heaven. Now, Hebrews tells us, the *leitourgia* is the eternal priestly service performed by Christ as the liturgist in heaven. Now something is taking place there that is a service, a ministry, performed on behalf of God's people on earth. As our liturgist in the heavenly sanctuary, Jesus Christ is the finisher of salvation. His resurrection and ascension were the beginning of His heavenly ministry *(leitourgia).*

[1]Theodore E. Tappert, ed., *The Book of Concord* (Philadelphia: Fortress Press, 1959), pp. 263–264.

This work of Christ in heaven takes place just prior to His second advent and the final judgment (Heb 9:21–28). It is a purifying and cleansing work. Therefore our worship, while it takes place in earthly sanctuaries, is not focused on what takes place there, but on what is taking place in heaven. It is this understanding of the heavenly ministry of our Lord that makes Adventist worship distinctive. Because Jesus is ministering in heaven we can enter there by faith now and in resurrection glory in the future. "Therefore, since we have such a great cloud of witnesses surrounding us, let us also lay aside every encumbrance, and the sin which so easily entangles us, and let us run with patience the race that is set before us, fixing our eyes on Jesus the author and perfector of faith, who for the joy that was set before Him endured the cross, despising the shame, and has sat down at the right hand of the throne of God" (Heb 12:1–2).

The focus of the Adventist Church in worship is on the heavenly sanctuary where Jesus, the Lord of the church, continually ministers as high priest in the heavenly liturgy, presenting before the Father His Calvary sacrifice. In response the heavenly beings, and the church on earth in its worship services, join in a never-ending glorification of the Godhead. "Let us, then, always offer praise to God as our sacrifice through Jesus, which is the offering presented by lips that confess Him as Lord" (Heb 13:15, TEV).

The Confident Approach

We do the final call of God an injustice, and the church and its members a disservice, if we read Rev 14:7 only evangelistically. It must be read pastorally, corporately, and liturgically as well. We have the task not only of persuading people that something cosmic and significant is happening in heaven, but also of helping them relate to that happening in dynamic personal and corporate worship. To convince people to make decisions for the Advent message and not to teach and train them to appreciate the connection between heavenly events and their worship is to fail completely. Such evangelism creates worshipers who do not know how to worship intelligently.

We have not paid enough attention to liturgical theology. We need to critically evaluate other churches' liturgical forms, but we also need to learn from and apply that which is right and good. In spite of our theological biblicism, when it comes to worship we are often rootless. This is not because there are no roots, but because we do not permit the roots to nourish the tree. We do not have a required form of worship, but that fact "can become a source of corruption if not informed with theological integrity."[2] Must maximum freedom result in minimum liturgical principles and training? Liturgical freedom, uninformed by theology, leads to mish-mash and hodge-podge, to a Sabbath morning minstral show, to pastoral prancing, and to theatricality. Worship becomes a form of religious entertainment. Whim and fancy play too large a role in determining what happens in our church services. It is strange that a church which prides itself on theological understanding and undergirding of the whole of life can put up with such a collection of liturgical litter. (By this I mean worship services that have been planned with little or no theological reflection on the meaning of the various parts.) Liturgically speaking we have ended up where we were never intended to be. The same concern was expressed by Norval Pease in the introduction to his book on worship:

> What is the answer to the problem of worship in our churches? It will not be found in ignoring the problem. If it is true that an enemy is trying to destroy the sacredness of Christian worship, we need to do something about it. Contentment with confusion, meaninglessness, and immaturity will not defeat this enemy. Neither will the answer be found in an uncritical acceptance of the procedures of some other churches. We are Adventists, and we must approach worship as Adventists. A worship service that meets the needs of Methodists, Episcopalians, or Presbyterians may be unsatisfactory for us. The answer will be found in (1) a thorough knowledge of the Biblical, theological, and historical aspects of Christian worship, and (2) a thoughtful application of this knowledge to Adventist worship today.[3]

It is because our conception of worship has been one-sided that we are faced with the present condition of worship in our church. Worship is dialectical in that it embodies both the transcendence and the immanence of God. Here our Western fear of the subjective comes to the surface. It is true, as Heppenstall says, that "there is a transcendent factor about the work of the Godhead in the heavenly sanctuary that must never be reduced to Christian experience, however important that may be."[4] But the problem for us is not one of reduction. It is the problem of relation. Does the worship that takes place in our churches on Sabbath morning have no relationship to the heavenly liturgy of our Lord? If it doesn't, then what are we doing there? If it does, what kind of relationship is it and what is it meant to do? Furthermore, how is it to be expressed in the order of service? If Rev 14:7 is a call

[2]Hoon, *The Integrity of Worship*, p. 15.

[3]Pease, *And Worship Him*, p. 8.

[4]Edward Heppenstall, *Christ Our High Priest* (Washington: Review and Herald Publishing Association, 1972), p. 23.

to worship, then we must ask *why*, *when*, and *how* are we to worship? *When* is answered by the seventh-day Sabbath. *Why* is answered christologically and eschatologically. *How* is answered liturgically.

Even though, as Heppenstall says, "The Christian does not find ultimate truth in himself,"[5] ultimate truth ought to have an effect on the Christian. Truth is not just a doctrine to be believed. Faith is not just a cerebral activity and response. Faith is also existential, ontological, as Ellen G. White recognizes in the following:

> Our God is a tender, merciful Father. His service should not be looked upon as a heart-saddening, distressing exercise. It should be a pleasure to worship the Lord and to take part in His work. God would not have His children, for whom so great salvation has been provided, act as if He were a hard, exacting taskmaster. He is their best friend; and when they worship Him, He expects to be with them, to bless and comfort them, filling their hearts with joy and love. The Lord desires His children to take comfort in His service, and to find more pleasure than hardship in His work. He desires that those who come to worship Him shall carry away with them precious thoughts of His love and care, that they may be cheered in all the employments of daily life, that they may have grace to deal honestly and faithfully in all things.[6]

God does not simply wait for man's response. The Bible indicates that God is responsive to man's condition and acts on man's behalf. It is when we recognize and accept God's acts on our behalf that we respond in worship and praise, and that kind of thankful response God does wait for and appreciate. His is not the kind of waiting that inhibits Him from acting sovereignly. It is, rather, the waiting of a lover who has loved and now anticipates the loved one to respond in kind.

What Jesus is doing in heaven is designed to give meaning to our existence in the last days, to help us understand our own being as creatures of the last days, and not just to provide interesting information. To be sure, "from the sanctuary God directs the battle to final victory,"[7] but once again that victory affects my life, my very existence, as well as my cerebrum, my thought processes. The transcendent factor in the work of Christ in heaven has a corresponding existential application. As a worshiper I am not simply an observer, a spectator. I am a participant. I am not standing on the outside looking in. That fact ought to have a determinative influence on our liturgical actions. The congregation is not an audience observing activities taking place on the

[5]Heppenstall, *Christ Our High Priest*, pp. 22–23.

[6]Ellen G. White, *Steps to Christ* (Mountain View, Calif.: Pacific Press Publishing Association, 1908), p. 103.

[7]Heppenstall, *Christ Our High Priest*, p. 23.

platform. Its members are participants, actively involved and engaged in corporate action in response to the revelation of God. As by faith they "remember" the cross of Calvary, so also they "remember" the events taking place now in heaven and enter there by faith. This is contemporary remembering as well as historical remembering.

The good news about the ministry of Christ in heaven is profitless unless it too is "united by faith in those who heard" (Heb 4:2). This does not mean that our faith determines what happens in heaven, or future events. But it does mean that apart from faith these events will profit us nothing as individuals and as a church.

The letter to the Hebrews invites believers to "draw near with confidence to the throne of grace" (Heb 4:16), where they can find the help they need, to "draw near to God through him" (Heb 7:25), to "come to Mt. Zion and to the city of the living God, the heavenly Jerusalem, and to myriads of angels, to the great assembly and church of the first-born who are enrolled in heaven, and to God the judge of all, and to the spirits of the righteous men made perfect, and to Jesus the mediator of a new covenant and to the sprinkled blood which speaks better than the blood of Abel" (Heb 12:22–24). How do we do this? By faith in worship! The outcome of such worship is assurance which makes the singing of the new song possible.

Hebrews 10 tells us that we have confidence to enter the heavenly sanctuary by the blood of Christ. Because of this we can enter by faith in boldness and assurance. Thus, as Peter Brunner writes, "The worship of the church has its place in the heavenly sanctuary, which was opened by Jesus' self-sacrifice; it has its place in the opened access to the Father. The worship of the church is freed for the performance of the celestial liturgy before God's throne," and is a "participation in the one world-redeeming, never ending worship of the crucified and exalted Christ before God's throne."[8] What a posture for the church of the last days: prostrate before the Father in its needs, yet coming into His presence boldly because Christ is its head and Master and Saviour! Surely it must be, as Richard Paquier suggests, "that something of the royal majesty and glory of the risen One who ascended into heaven has to come through in the worship of the church."[9] The royal glory of Christ must be permitted to shine through in the church's liturgical action in worship. In all that it says and does in worship the church is proclaiming to the whole world, and to itself, that the Lord reigns in heaven and is in its midst by the Holy Spirit. The church in which

[8]Brunner, *Worship in the Name of Jesus*, p. 79.
[9]Paquier, *Dynamics of Worship*, p. 22.

Christ is present by His Holy Spirit is portrayed in Revelation as Mount Zion and the 144,000. The ultimate aim of this church's worship is "that at the name of Jesus every knee should bow, in heaven and on the earth and under the earth, and every tongue confess that Jesus Christ is Lord, to the glory of God the Father" (Phil 2:10).

In the final great worship service God's plan of salvation will be vindicated. This vindication is reflected, though imperfectly and in anticipation, in the church's worship on earth each Sabbath. Henry Sloan Coffen wrote: "A congregation assembled for worship comes together on certain assumptions, and he who leads them should respect the mutual basis on which he and they meet. They are not there to listen to the ideas of a speaker, however interesting, but to share the heritage of the church of all the christian centuries."[10] This is especially true of the church of the last days. It meets for worship on the assumption that God has called and gathered His people together and is addressing them from the heavenly sanctuary by means of His Word, for the purpose of fortifying them in their hope and strengthening them in their mission. That confrontation in worship between God and His people is the greatest thing that can ever happen! Such worship gives life.

Worship is the lifeblood, the heartbeat, of the last-day church. It is essential for its life and mission. If *this* church does not worship it will soon disappear in spite of its institutions and programs. The Adventist believer is obliged to worship. No Sabbath should pass without attendance at the main worship service of the church. As Adventist believers we need to remember that we will never reach the point, on this side of the resurrection, when we can live without receiving from the Lord. Worship is the grateful acceptance of His gifts of grace which sustain and give power for faithful service. No worship service gets its significance from the spiritual assets of the worshipers. Biblical faith rests from its own works and waits for the works of God. Such faith will learn what it means to worship God.

The Cleansed Conscience

As worship is the great issue in the great controversy and in the events of the heavenly sanctuary, so it is also the major activity of the church. The last-day church has been called into being to worship the Creator God and glorify the Lamb of God who takes away the sin of the world. The work of this church is worship. Worship is its major activity. Worship is the focus of its life and energy. Its mission is to invite

[10]Henry Sloan Coffen, *Communion Through Preaching* (New York: Scribner, 1952), p. 105.

all people everywhere to join in this worship, because "Jesus had come to teach the meaning of the worship of God."[11]

The worship of the last-day church is not only possible but central because Jesus is alive and seated at the right hand of the Father. A seated High Priest is the guarantee of a finished work and an accepted sacrifice. From the shame of the cross He has been exalted to the highest authority and glory. That is why we are able to come confidently into His presence to avail ourselves of His high priestly ministry. In Him we have access to all the grace and power of God. To all who think they are unworthy to come into His presence comes the word that we have a High Priest who entered heaven with His own blood to plead that blood before the Father on our behalf. His blood is the assurance we will be dealt with graciously (Heb 10:19–25).

Under the old covenant the people did not have the privilege of entering the Holy Place or the Most Holy Place in the tabernacle or temple. Only the priest could do that. The high priest could only enter the Most Holy Place once each year and not any time he chose. When he did enter he was the representative of the people. They could not enter at all. Under the new covenant we believers have free access to the Father because Jesus not only opened the way but has gone there as a forerunner on our behalf. He has literally opened the way into the heavenly sanctuary for us. In worship, and by faith, we enter the heavenly sanctuary freely and without hindrance.

What is it that most hinders a free and spontaneous and joyful expression of worship? What is it that keeps us from experiencing the greatest joys of worship? Is it not a sense of guilt? Even after we have become believers and accepted the truth about Jesus and His sacrifice we still feel in some strange sense unworthy to come into God's presence. Every pastor is aware that some of his people find it difficult to participate in the Lord's Supper because of a continuing sense of sin and guilt. But the Seventh-day Adventist ought to have a special insight into the freedom of the gospel, into the freedom of worship, into open access to the throne of God, into acceptance and assurance. Heppenstall says:

> By virtue of His priestly work Christ binds believers into fellowship with the Father. We are separated from God as sinners. We require someone who has access to the throne of God. We stand daily in need of priestly intervention. Through Christ we approach God in perfect trust. The believers are so complete in Christ that in Him they have fellowship with the Father and the Son. The Father beholds them in

[11]Ellen G. White, *The Desire of Ages* (Mountain View, Calif.: Pacific Press Publishing Association, 1898), p. 84.

> His Son. He sees that they are one with His Son and therefore one with the Father. They now stand in the same relationship to the Father as does the Lord Jesus Christ. They are sons of God. God loves them as He loves His Son. Nothing can separate us from the love of God (see Romans 8:38–39).[12]

The Bible says: "Since we have a great priest over the house of God, let us draw near with a sincere heart with full assurance of faith, having our hearts sprinkled clean from an evil conscience and our body washed with pure water" (Heb 10:21–22). What beautiful language! What a beautiful experience! It ought to be reflected in our worship. We are that kind of people, the redeemed of God. When we know His inward cleansing, then we can come into His presence in full assurance of faith.

The greatest thing a person can experience is a clean conscience. It is the conscience that condemns. It is the guilty conscience that hinders a person from joy and happiness, that keeps him from truly worshiping God. A guilty conscience hinders a grateful appreciation of the Lord's Supper. It tells us that we are sinners, and we would rather listen to our conscience than to the gospel. Conscience can be a tyrant, telling us over and over again that we are guilty sinners with no hope, that no matter what God's Word says our Lord is doing for us in heaven, we are still guilty and condemned. But that is a deceived conscience speaking.

God has given the human conscience a perfect standard by which to judge itself: His law. Through the conscience His law functions inwardly and produces a sense of guilt in the inner man. That is good and needful. But God also sprinkles us clean from an evil conscience. Worship under the old covenant was designed to bring people into the presence of God. But it was a shadowy, imperfect kind of worship. The people came with their guilty consciences and wanted release. They offered sacrifices, but many lacked spiritual insight into the meaning of those sacrifices. Their rituals only served the "purification of the flesh" (Heb 9:13). They received an outward, symbolic cleansing and not a real, experiential, inward cleansing. In spite of the symbols, their consciences could still condemn them. Ceremonially cleansed, the worshiper could still feel far away from God. The barrier to ritual worship was removed, but the door to God's presence was shut for many and the heart could still be heavy.

It is the blood of Christ which He took into the heavenly sanctuary which cleanses and makes clean the conscience. There is only one way

[12]Heppenstall, *Christ Our High Priest*, p. 67.

for something dirty to be made clean, and that is by the removal of the dirt. The only way the human conscience can be made clean is by the removal of the sin which it recognizes and which condemns the sinner. God does not deal only with our guilt. He deals with our sin. His method is to "put away sin by the sacrifice of himself" (Heb 9:26). Is there anything we can do to cleanse and purify our conscience? Nothing at all! No resolution, no ritual, will suffice. This cleansing takes an act of God, an act of grace. Jesus does for us what we cannot do for ourselves. First, He deals with sin by dying for sin. Then He puts away sin by removing all record of it from the heavenly sanctuary (Dan 8:14, Rev 5:1–13). There is now no record to stand against us any more! If there is nothing to stand against us, nothing to accuse us, our conscience cannot condemn us when God Himself does not.[13]

The Word says that Christ's blood purifies the conscience from "dead works." What are "dead works"? They are the useless things we try to do to merit God's favor or to satisfy our guilty conscience, but which do not relieve the conscience. But if we believe and trust in the sacrifice of Christ and His ministry in heaven on our behalf, we won't bother with any of these dead works. We will instead rest in Him. "Good works" are the spontaneous acts of love that issue from a purified conscience. If our conscience condemns us after he has forgiven our sins and cleansed us from all unrighteousness, it is because we do not believe. What we lack is faith. If God says our sins are forgiven and wiped from the record, and we refuse to believe it and continue with a condemning conscience, then our conscience is not our guide. It has instead become our god and that god is a tyrant. It will never give us the peace we need and want so badly. When Jesus blots the record in heaven our conscience is being made clean! The gospel, the good news, is that the grace of God has triumphed over sin and made us free. The Bible says:

> If the worshippers had once been cleansed, they would no longer have any consciousness of sin. But in these sacrifices there is a reminder of sin year after year. For it is impossible that the blood of bulls and goats should *take away* sins. . . . We have been sanctified through the offering of the body of Jesus Christ once for all . . . for by a single offering he has perfected for all time those who are being sanctified (Heb 10: 2–4, 10, 14, emphasis mine).

Praise God! That's why Adventists worship. We have access to the Father. Sin is being removed. Our consciences are clean. It is like being "washed with pure water." What refreshment there is in taking a bath

[13]See Heppenstall, *Christ Our High Priest*, chapters 6 and 9.

in clean, flowing water when we are sweaty and dirty! It is uplifting and exhilarating. Worship for the Seventh-day Adventist, whose focus is on the heavenly sanctuary, ought to have the same result. By faith we enter the sanctuary in full confidence and there we see that no sin stands against us. Our consciences no longer condemn us; we are free, and we rejoice in praise to the Father and the Son, who have done it all for us.

Should not this joyous message of the heavenly sanctuary be reflected in our liturgy? If anything would cause God's people to sing the song of freedom and faith it is this message of completed redemption.

Discussion Questions

1. If the essence of worship is faith and obedience, what role do they play in both the individual and corporate experience of worship?
2. In what way is the fundamental issue of the great controversy reflected in both the individual and corporate experience of worship?
3. Why is it essential that the focus of SDA worship be on events now taking place in the heavenly sanctuary rather than on what takes place in church sanctuaries on Sabbath?
4. How is it possible to reflect the focus on the heavenly sanctuary in the liturgy of the worship service?

Worship and the Second Advent / 6

In its worship the Seventh-day Adventist Church not only looks back in grateful memory, but also looks forward in confident hope. That hope rests firmly on the biblical promises concerning the imminent return of the Lord Jesus Christ. Adventist worship takes place, therefore, on the threshold of His coming.

A Forward Look

Heb 10:25 admonishes the church not to forsake "our own assembling together, as is the habit of some, but encouraging one another; and all the more as you see the Day drawing near." The "Day" is obviously a reference to the final appearance of the Lord Jesus Christ, His return to earth to claim His bride, the church, and take his church to be with Him forever. In Adventist worship the three time dimensions of human existence are engaged. We have not only the theology that is foundational to such an experience, we have also the responsibility to make it a reality liturgically. The significance of the Sabbath, as the church exercises its historical memory, satisfies our need to go back in faith to the beginning, to our roots, to the One who created all things. By faith we also enter the heavenly sanctuary to share in the great events taking place there that will determine the future history of the world as well as our own personal histories. By that entrance our present need to maintain a faith connection with the ministry of Christ our High Priest is satisfied. It is as we look toward the future with hope in the completion of that heavenly priestly work and in the return of our Lord that our need for assurance with respect to the future is met.

The past we can do nothing about, though it may haunt us. The present is here now and we have some control over its events, so it holds little threat for us. But the future is something else. The future threatens because it represents the unknown and the uncertain. What will tomorrow bring? It is here that the message concerning the second advent of our Lord is such a blessing to His people. In prophetic wisdom the Bible tells us what can be expected in the future. The future will not come as a horrible surprise for believing people. They, at least, will not be caught unprepared for the final great events of history.

It is in anticipation of that day that the church of the present worships. Its focus is not only on the past great events of history, nor on present events that will determine history in the sanctuary above, but on the fulfillment of God's Word in future historical events. "For our citizenship is in heaven, from which also we eagerly wait for a Saviour, the Lord Jesus Christ; who will transform the body of our humble state into conformity with the body of His glory, by the exertion of the power that He has even to subject all things to Himself" (Phil 3:20–21). And the apostle Peter wrote: "Since all these are to be destroyed in this way, what sort of people ought you to be in holy conduct and godliness, looking for and hastening the coming of the day of God, on account of which the heavens will be destroyed by burning, and the elements will melt with intense heat. But according to his promise we are looking for new heavens and a new earth, in which righteousness dwells" (2 Pet 3:11–13). It doesn't take much reading in the Bible to realize, as Hoon says, that "eschatology is the dominant mode of New Testament worship and the key that unlocks its normative meaning."[1]

Worship in Anticipation

The worship of the New Testament church took place in anticipation of the Lord's return. The early church believed in His early return, and that expectation is reflected in its worship. In the introduction to his book *Worship in the New Testament*, Gerhard Delling makes the following observation:

> The coming of Christ can only be awaited by christians. One can only be a christian through being joined to Christ. To be joined to Christ means to live by the cross and resurrection, to live in the presence of Christ, to live for the coming of Christ, and that means for the primitive church . . . to hold services. Their celebrations meant living by the saving deeds of Christ in fellowship with the risen One in the expectation of His Parousia. Obviously if the service of the present time can be understood in some sense as a kind of anticipation of the final

[1]Hoon, *The Integrity of Worship*, p. 350.

> service, it is indispensable for a church which expects the end soon: today when the era of salvation has begun, it does—even if in a preliminary way—what it will do tomorrow in the final fulfillment. Hence there is no possibility of being christian in the New Testament without worship.[2]

One might make that statement even more specific to our context and say that it is not possible to be a Seventh-day Adventist Christian living in the last days without worship. Ellen G. White wrote: "To the humble, believing soul, the house of God on earth is the gate of heaven. The song of praise, the prayer, the words spoken by Christ's representatives, are God's appointed agencies to prepare a people for the church above, for that loftier worship in which there can enter nothing that defileth."[3] Our worship "should be pervaded with the very atmosphere of heaven."[4]

Though the church is now here in the present world and under the present circumstances, its worship has a definite eschatological orientation. In its worship the last-day church leaves itself behind and reaches out toward that consummation which transcends the confines of time and space. It could be said that in its worship the church is already at that moment in time when Jesus appears. His church has gathered to meet Him. It could be said that every Sabbath the worship of the church is its rehearsal for the day of the Lord when He shall appear in fact. In the prayers, the preaching, the hymn singing, the church is rehearsing for the day when it will see Him and speak with Him face to face, when it will hear the divine Word from the Word Himself, when it will sing the sanctus and doxology in everlasting praise of the Lamb who was slain and is worthy to receive worship and acclaim. The worship of the last-day church is taking place at that point in time when the world is passing away and the new world of God is about to come. In its worship the last-day church is on tip-toe, on the edge of its seat, on the threshold, eager to see and hear the Lord. In faith it reaches out to welcome Him. What it says and does on the Sabbath is in anticipation of that great day. It is a foretaste of the great event.

That is why the worship of the last-day church takes place in the context of Revelation 14. Acknowledging the seventh-day Sabbath as the Lord's Day, conscious of entering by faith into the sanctuary above, and anticipating the Lord's imminent return, it feeds on His

[2]Gerhard Delling, *Worship in the New Testament* (Philadelphia: Westminster Press, 1962), p. xii.

[3]White, *Testimonies for the Church*, Vol. 5, p. 491.

[4]Ibid., p. 609.

Word and the sacraments and goes forth to proclaim salvation in Him alone. It is interested and involved, not only in past and present history, but in the climax of history as well. It has an *adventist* theory about the development of historical events. The world is God's, this theory says. He made it. He is in it. But the world has thwarted His purposes. Soon He will arrive in judgment and redemption. History will conclude with Christ's second coming. That is our hope. Our hope is not in the best that fallen mankind is able to produce. Our hope is in what God has done and is doing and will do. The worship of the last-day church is positive and hopeful and forward-looking in the midst of negative thinking and hopeless modern existence. Emil Brunner has said:

> What oxygen is for the lungs, such is hope for the meaning of human life. Take oxygen away and death occurs through suffocation, take hope away and humanity is constricted through lack of breath; despair supervenes, spelling the paralysis of intellectual and spiritual powers by a feeling of senselessness and purposelessness of existence. As the fate of the human organism is dependent on the supply of oxygen, so the fate of humanity is dependent on its supply of hope.[5]

Worship in the Interim

The Christian church is an eschatological phenomenon, born in the end times for an end-time life and an end-time mission with an end-time message. The worship of that end-time church is also an eschatological phenomenon. The last-day church is set apart from the world and has been integrated into Christ's body, and it gathers in its worship to give visible and audible expression to its anticipation of the coming of its Lord. In the interval between His ascension and His return the church worships. It was not coincidental that the disciples held a prayer meeting right after the message concerning the Lord's return was given. "It was not long afterwards that He arose into the sky and disappeared into a cloud, leaving them staring after Him. As they were straining their eyes for another glimpse, suddenly two white robed men were standing there among them, and said, 'Men of Galilee, why are you standing here staring at the sky? Jesus has gone away to heaven, and some day, just as He went, He will return!' They were at the Mount of Olives when this happened, so now they walked the half mile back to Jerusalem and held a prayer meeting in an upstairs room of the house where they were staying" (Acts 1:9–12).

Is there any activity that better befits the life of the church as it waits for the second coming? Worship *is* waiting. In worship the

[5]Emil Brunner, *Eternal Hope* (Philadelphia: Westminster Press, 1954), p. 7.

church waits for the return of its Lord. But in worship it also moves toward and prepares for that great event. The preparation of the church for that day is far different from the world's. Through the ministry of the Holy Spirit in word and sacrament the Lord is preparing the church to meet Him with joy. The world, on the other hand, is preparing itself for judgment by its continuous rebellion and sin. As the church is getting ready for redemption and glory, the world is getting ready for judgment and death. This hastening of the church, and the world, toward the second advent takes place primarily as the church worships. It is in the bowed knee that the church publicly confesses its faith in God, its dependence upon Him, and its expectation of His coming again.

The worship of the last-day church expresses its deep longing for its heavenly home. The church is very much aware that it can worship only fragmentarily and incompletely and it longs for that time when it will be able to worship in heavenly splendor. It knows its worship is feeble and even distorted at best, and it waits for the day when it will be able to magnify God with all the angels and heavenly beings in everlasting praise and thanksgiving. Thus in worship, says von Allmen, "There is an overlapping of the age to come and the present age; though we are no longer of the world we are still in it."[6] Taking place on the Sabbath and signifying rest by faith in the completed work of redemption, conscious of the gracious work of Christ in heaven, the worship of the last-day church is portrayed in Heb 12:22–29. In worship the church comes to Mount Zion, the heavenly dwelling place of God. As the earthly Zion, Jerusalem, was the meeting place for the tribes of Israel, so heavenly Zion is the meeting place for the church. As the people of God will be gathered by the Lord with Jesus in their midst on the day of His appearing, they anticipate that event by a weekly gathering all over the world (Rev 14:1).

We are a pilgrim people *in via* toward Zion. But on the basis of God's sure promise we have arrived there by faith as we look forward to the future. We do not have to climb great heights to reach Him. He is accessible to every believer. He has made His dwelling place in our midst by His Spirit. In our worship we join the angelic worshipers in praise of the King in our midst who will soon come in person.

We are a part of the great assembly of God's people the world over, the church of the first-born. We became members by the new birth. We are now part of the communion of saints and are enrolled as

[6]Jean Jacques von Allmen, *Preaching and Congregation* (Richmond, Va.: John Knox Press, 1962), p. 36.

citizens of heaven. Though earthbound, our home is in heaven where Jesus is. God is our refuge and by virtue of Christ we can have with Him a relationship of intimacy mixed with awe because of His pure holiness and our consciousness that He is the judge of all. We join our prayers and praise of God with those of all righteous people everywhere, all who have been born again.

We come to Jesus as the Mediator between God and man, and because of His sprinkled blood our consciences are clean. The removal of the sin that stands against us does away with the barrier between us and the Father. When we worship we hear God address His church directly from the throne in heaven through the preaching of the Word and the ministry of the Holy Spirit. The God whom we worship is not silent. He has a will for His people and He communicates that will as His church keeps silence before Him and listens. His Word is not disregarded by His church as it was by the Israelites after Sinai. God's purpose is declared. He will shake the earth and the heavens. Presumably this shaking includes His church. As we worship we are aware that our response is crucial with respect to the shaking of the last days. If we refuse to heed Him and obey we will be shaken out. While our relationship with God is free and intimate, based on gospel, it is still a fearful thing to fall into the hands of the living God. He will have His will prevail. We worship a God who is powerful and almighty. The entire universe will be shaken to pieces and only that will survive which is unshakable. To the unshakable belongs the kingdom which believers in Christ share with Him. The kingdom that we have received by faith and in grace is unshakable, and for that we rejoice. Our thankfulness is profoundly expressed in joyful worship.

The proper response to the grace of God is a grateful heart. The words and actions which flow from a grateful heart are the sacrifices in which God delights. Such worship is given with a sense of the majesty and holiness of God the Judge with whom we have to do. But this sense of His majesty, this reverence and awe, does not make His people flee from Him, for they are the redeemed. Their way has been opened; a place is being prepared for them and they are being prepared for that place. This reverence and awe cause His people to "come," to "draw near"—like metal irresistibly drawn to a magnet. Such is the worship of the last-day church on the threshold of the Lord's return.

The worship of the last-day church is a foretaste of the final gathering on Mount Zion when Jesus comes again. A feeling of expectation should permeate our worship services, and, consequently, there should be much praise in our liturgy. With praise the church sings the new song of the redeemed for itself and for the world so that the whole world can learn to sing it too.

Discussion Questions

1. Is it possible to live as a Christian during the end times without both individual and corporate worship? If not, why not?
2. In what ways does the worship of the end-times church constitute a rehearsal of the events connected with Christ's return?

Worship and the Sacraments / 7

It is necessary at the outset of this chapter to say a few words about the use of the term "sacrament." The fact that Ellen White uses it quite freely, as well as the term "ordinance" (see *Desire of Ages*, chapter 72), ought to demonstrate its legitimacy for Adventists. However, "sacrament" has come to mean, in the minds of many, the somewhat magical mystique of the Roman Catholic mass, particularly in reference to the transubstantiation doctrine of the Lord's Supper, and thus it has acquired a negative connotation. Is this reputation deserved? Is the word "sacrament" valid for Adventist usage?

It is helpful to recall that the Latin *sacramentum*, from which we derive "sacrament," was a rendering of the Greek *musterion* (mystery). For a long while both terms were used interchangeably for any ritual observance of the church, most often for baptism and the Lord's Supper. In Latin usage *sacramentum* referred to a pledge or solemn oath by which two parties were bound legally. Sometimes it included the transfer of earnest money as a sacramental pledge. It later found its way into Christian theological language, along with many other secular terms, and began to acquire new meaning. We are much better able to use it if we retain the essence of its original meaning as a simple reference to the covenant relationship between God and His people. In this sense "sacrament" simply expresses the mutual pledge of that relationship and thus is not at all incompatible with Adventist beliefs. Our alternate term "ordinance" came into usage through Puritanism, for which the term "sacrament" was too superstitious.

Along with the majority of Protestant churches, Seventh-day Adventists consider baptism and the Lord's Supper to be the two biblical sacraments. We believe we follow the traditions of early Christianity, which divided corporate worship into two liturgical parts: the liturgy of the Word, and the liturgy of the upper room. We see ourselves participating in what James F. White calls "signs of a developing recognition of the centrality of the Church's worship in shaping its witness and mission to the world."[1] This chapter is intended to focus the reader's attention on the value of sacramental worship.

Baptism

One of the most important statements on baptism in the New Testament is Rom 6:1–11.

> What shall we say then? Shall we go on sinning so that grace may increase? By no means! We died to sin; how can we live in it any longer? Or don't you know that all of us who were baptized into Christ Jesus were baptized into his death? We were therefore buried with him through baptism into death in order that, just as Christ was raised from the dead through the glory of the Father, we too may live a new life. If we have been united with him in his death, we will certainly also be united with him in his resurrection. For we know that our old self was crucified with him so that the body of sin might be rendered powerless, that we should no longer be slaves to sin—because anyone who has died has been freed from sin. Now if we died with Christ, we believe that we will also live with him. For we know that since Christ was raised from the dead, he cannot die again; death no longer has mastery over him. The death he died, he died to sin once for all; but the life he lives he lives to God. In the same way, count yourselves dead to sin but alive to God in Christ Jesus (NIV).

Paul tells us that baptism signifies death, burial, and resurrection. This has significant implications for contemporary baptismal practices.

Baptism: A Sign of Death and Burial

The trend in the Adventist church is to baptize at an ever-earlier age. Will the day finally arrive when we begin to practice infant baptism and replace the flood that washes with a trickle that tickles? Is our practice of baptism already in danger of being nothing more than a recognition ceremony for having arrived at a transitional point in life, a rite of passage rather than of separation from the world and inclusion into a radically new society? The way baptism is often practiced would lead one to conclude it is not very important either to candidate or church. So often it is simply stuck in somewhere in the worship service with little or no reference to surrounding liturgical elements. In fact

[1]James F. White, *Sacraments as God's Self-Giving* (Nashville: Abingdon, 1983), p. 9.

one is in danger of missing it entirely by a momentary distraction. The curtain of the baptistry is whisked open, the candidate is dunked, and the curtain is whisked shut again before one can blink twice. Such a careless practice needs liturgical reformation if baptism is to be experienced by candidate and church as a dramatic event, one that dramatizes belief. The trend toward earlier baptism needs examination in the light of the relationship between baptism and discipleship.

This is especially crucial for a church that places a high premium on Christian education. As vital as Christian education is, the church does not grow by osmosis or by progressive learning. It grows by conversion. The goal of a parochial education is not the teaching of Christian morals and ethics alone. The goal of Christian education is to make Christians, disciples, who are related to the Lord by faith--the goal is conversion, " . . . the work of redemption. This is the object of education, the great object of life."[2]

"I tell you the truth," said Jesus, "unless a man is born again, he cannot see the kingdom of God" (John 3:3, NIV). Baptism is part of the born-again experience, as Jesus says in the same chapter: "I tell you the truth, unless a man is born of water and the Spirit, he cannot enter the kingdom of God" (3:5, NIV). The clear impression is given that this is an adult experience, that is to say, the individual must be able to make an intelligent, mature decision knowing full well its implications. If it is true that "we need converted ministers,"[3] it is even more true that the church needs converted members. In fact, the true church has no other kind.

Biblical baptism, immersion, is the most appropriate symbol for what should actually be taking place in the candidate's spiritual experience: death, burial, renunciation of the old life, and the start of a new life—a radically new beginning. It signifies an about-face, a new direction, the conscious and deliberate turning away from a life of sin. It means submission. It means to have a new Boss. In fact, in Jesus' view of the spiritual experience of rebirth, baptism comes before teaching and learning (Matt 28:19–20), but not before faith: "Whoever believes and is baptized will be saved, but whoever does not believe will be condemned" (Mark 16:16, NIV). This does not mean to baptize and then teach the baptized to have faith. It means to baptize one who has heard and learned the gospel, has repented, believes, and now desires to surrender to the lordship of Christ. Only then can he/she be taught

[2]Ellen G. White, *Education* (Mountain View, Calif: Pacific Press Publishing Association, 1903), p. 16.

[3]White, *Testimonies for the Church*, Vol. 4, p. 315.

by the Holy Spirit and learn to produce the fruits of the Spirit. Conversion makes it possible for a person to *be* right, not just think right.

Jesus spoke of His impending death on the cross as His baptism, and said to His disciples, "You will drink the cup I drink and be baptized with the baptism I am baptized with" (Mark 10:38–39, NIV). His water baptism by John was the first step toward the cross, the beginning of a direct route from the Jordan to Calvary. Cross, death, and baptism are intertwined in Christ's life. The same is true for the Christian. This is why Dietrich Bonhoeffer was able to say, and to live, these words: "When Christ calls a man He bids him come and die."[4] The baptismal candidate must face the question of whether or not he/she is ready and willing to accept, and pay, the cost of discipleship.

Even the downward plunge into the baptismal water is a dramatic liturgical symbol of death and burial, which cannot be adequately symbolized by sprinkling or pouring. What is at issue is the relationship between the symbolic action in baptism, and belief. If we believe that baptism signifies death and burial, then immersion is the only adequate liturgical illustration of that belief. What the church believes about baptism will be dramatized in what it does when it baptizes.

Just as in physical death life ceases, so baptism signifies that the old life of willful sin comes to an end. This "life," as we call it, was really not life at all; it was more a living death. In many ways the life of sin is comparable to death. It is a life of darkness and separation from God, just as death is darkness and the grave separates. The dead are at the mercy of the decaying process, of corruption, and so it is with the life of sin. The dead cannot speak, cannot move, cannot think. They cannot exercise the power of will. They have no breath, no heartbeat, no strength, no hope. What could be more descriptive of the unrepentant, unconverted state?

The life of sin is a downward march toward death, either physical death or the death to sin that accompanies spiritual rebirth. It is this latter death that is dramatized in baptism. In physical death all that meant life comes to an end. In Christian baptism all that was a part of the life of sin comes to an end. The old passes away so that all can become new (2 Cor 5:17). The baptized person lives as though dead, as one who has given up and let go, who has succumbed to an end. "Baptism is a most solemn renunciation of the world. Self is by profession dead to a life of sin. The waters cover the candidate, and in the presence of the whole heavenly universe the mutual pledge is made. In

[4]Dietrich Bonhoeffer, *The Cost of Discipleship*, trans. R. H. Fuller (New York: The Macmillan Company, 1957), p. 73.

the name of the Father, the Son, and the Holy Spirit, man is laid in his watery grave, buried with Christ in baptism, and raised from the water to live the new life of loyalty to God."[5]

Baptism signifies the end of self-centered and self-directed living. The candidate falls in step with the life of the church. He/she is part of a new society that does not function in the same way as the secular, materialistic, and immoral world. The apostle Paul had a lot to say concerning church members who are disruptive, non-supportive, divisive troublemakers (Rom 6:1–2, 13–14, 13:1–14; 1 Cor 1:10–12, 3:16–23, 5:1–13, 6:9–11; Eph 4:1–32, 5:1–33; Col 3:1–25; 1 Thess 4:1–12; 1 John 3:9–10). In the baptismal rite of some denominations the candidate is asked: "Do you renounce the devil, and all his works, and all his ways?" The candidate is expected to answer, "I renounce them." In churches that practice confirmation the confirmand who has been catechized (taught the gospel and the meaning of discipleship) is asked the same question in a reaffirmation of earlier baptismal vows. Such questions focus on the fact that baptism does not signify simply acceptance of the candidate just as he/she is. It signifies, instead, a change of direction, of allegiance, and of service. It is only when a person is dead to sin and alive in Christ that he is free to be a Christian. Dead people cannot sin, and those who are dead to sin and alive in Christ will not to sin. "We died to sin," said Paul; "how can we live in it any longer?" (Rom 6:2, NIV). As William Willimon says, "The gospel call as signified in baptism is much more radical and painful than a mere 'Be clean!' It is: *You will be made dead!*"[6]

Baptism: A Sign of Resurrection and New Life

Baptism obliges the church to make clear in its preaching and teaching the distinction between living like a pagan and living like a converted Christian, a distinction made vivid by Peter, who wrote:

> Therefore, since Christ suffered in his body, arm yourselves also with the same attitude, because he who has suffered in his body is done with sin. As a result, he does not live the rest of his earthly life for evil human desires, but rather for the will of God. For you have spent enough time in the past doing what pagans choose to do—living in debauchery, lust, drunkenness, orgies, carousing and detestable idolatry. They think it strange that you do not plunge with them into the same flood of dissipation, and they heap abuse on you. But they

[5]Ellen G. White, *Seventh-day Adventist Bible Commentary*, Vol. 6 (Washington: Review and Herald Publishing Association, 1957), p. 1074.

[6]William H. Willimon, *The Service of God* (Nashville: Abingdon, 1983), p. 99.

will have to give account to him who is ready to judge the living and the dead. For this is the reason the gospel was preached even to those who are now dead, so that they might be judged according to men in regard to the body, but live according to God in regard to the spirit (1 Pet 4:1–6, NIV).

The catechetical instruction that leads to faith prior to baptism must become more rigorous as society becomes more pagan. Furthermore, the church must not hesitate to make clear the moral and ethical expectations of God for the converted life. Failure to do so constitutes heresy of a fundamental nature. Paul wrote: "Do not let sin reign in your mortal body so that you obey its evil desires. Do not offer the parts of your body to sin, as instruments of wickedness, but rather offer yourselves to God, as those who have been brought from death to life; and offer the parts of your body to him as instruments of righteousness" (Rom 6:12–13, NIV). Also: "Christ loved the church and gave himself up for her to make her holy, cleansing her by the washing with water through the word, and to present her to himself as a radiant church, without stain or wrinkle or any other blemish, but holy and blameless" (Eph 5:25–27, NIV). Those who have been washed in baptism no longer live as the sexually immoral, idolaters, adulterers, prostitutes, homosexuals, thieves, drunkards, slanderers, swindlers, or greedy—for such will not inherit the kingdom of God. "And that is what some of you were. But you were washed, you were sanctified, you were justified in the name of the Lord Jesus Christ and by the Spirit of our God" (1 Cor 6:9–11, NIV). Furthermore, the ethical demands of the gospel are outlined by Jesus in Matthew 25:34ff. These are the marks of the converted Christian: he/she feeds the hungry, gives drink to the thirsty, provides lodging for the homeless, clothes the naked, takes care of the sick, and visits those who are imprisoned.

It is obvious that the life of the baptized is in harmony with God's expectations. Of those baptized whose lives do not give evidence of such harmony, Ellen White says, "They have been baptized, but they were buried alive. Self did not die, and therefore they did not rise to newness of life in Christ."[7]

The baptized convert is to live a life of holiness, not of autonomous, independent, individualistic doing of one's own religious thing. The baptized person is to be consecrated to a God-directed and obedient life of worship and service. Such obedience is learned through suffering and death (Heb 5:8). There is a cross in Christianity. Therefore, Christian discipleship is not made up of resolutions but of a

[7]White, *Seventh-day Adventist Bible Commentary*, Vol. 6, p. 1075.

daily dying of the old life of sin, and a daily resurrection of the new life in Christ.

The baptized believer will not willfully sin, but because of the new relationship with Jesus he/she has an advocate when sins are committed, as Peter says: "My dear children, I write this to you so that you will not sin. But if anybody does sin, we have one who speaks to the Father in our defense—Jesus Christ the Righteous One" (1 John 2:1).

As baptism signifies the death of the old life of sin and rebellion against God, it also signifies the new life of faith and trust in the Lord, obedience to His will, and self-forgetful service to God and man. Of Jesus Paul said, "The death he died, he died to sin once for all, but the life he lives he lives to God. In the same way, count yourselves dead to sin but alive to God in Christ Jesus. Therefore do not let sin reign in your mortal body so that you obey its evil desires" (Rom 6:10–12, NIV). Having been plunged into the watery grave, the candidate is pulled up out of that grave to a whole new existence. One does not baptize himself any more than one buries himself. One is plunged into the water and pulled forth. It is a foretaste of that experience when, at Christ's coming and at the sound of the trumpet, He will call us from our graves, from eternal death to eternal life. "I tell you the truth, whoever hears my word and believes him who sent me has eternal life and will not be condemned; he has crossed over from death to life. I tell you the truth, a time is coming and now has come when the dead will hear the voice of the Son of God and those who hear will live" (John 5:24–25; see also verses 28–29).

Baptism is the first step in the new life of faith and obedience, and as such signifies discipleship. A disciple is one who lives a disciplined life, has put himself under subjection and under the discipline of the Holy Spirit. "Do you not know that your body is a temple of the Holy Spirit who is in you, whom you have from God, and that you are not your own? For you have been bought with a price: therefore glorify God in your body. . . . do not become slaves of men" (1 Cor 6:19–20, 7:23, NAS). The baptized believer is truly one possessed—possessed by the Lord! a slave of Christ! "He who was called while free, is Christ's slave" (1 Cor 7:22b, NAS). To be free in Christ does not mean to live as one pleases, which is called licentiousness in Scripture (a misuse of Christian freedom), but to be set free from the power of sin, devil, and the carnal nature that keeps one from living according to the will of God. The believer is now free for faith and obedience, free to live a God-pleasing life. As Bonhoeffer puts it: "The only man who has the right to say that he is justified by grace alone is the man who has left all to follow Christ."[8]

For the baptized God provides the spiritual resources to meet every spiritual need and sustain the believer in the maintenance of the new relationship and the new life. Baptism seals the relationship, which is then cultivated by the Word and the ministry of the Holy Spirit as the newly baptized participates in the worship life of the new community, the church, of which he/she is now a part. In this connection the weekly Sabbath is an opportunity established by God in perpetuity for a renewal of initial surrender and a recommitment of life to Him.[9] This provision is part of God's grace so that the dying and rising of baptism can continue until glory is reached at last.

The significance of baptism does not come alone from the symbolism described above, nor from the knowledge of what it means to be dead to sin and alive to God. It comes also from the fact that God acts in baptism; He has taken the initiative. Baptism is more than a public witness by the candidate to the experience of conversion. It is also a witness by God to His act of grace in claiming the baptized as His own. "The three great powers in heaven are witnesses; they are invisible but present" at baptism. For what purpose? "Let those who received the imprint of God by baptism [remember] that upon them the Lord has placed His signature, declaring them to be His sons and daughters."[10] The point is that baptism is an act of God as well as of the candidate and of the church.

This says something about the handling of baptism during the worship service. The baptismal rite itself should be theocentric, not just anthropocentric. Scriptures should be read and words spoken that call attention, not only to the candidate's decision and witness, but also to the grace and mercy of God who has brought the candidate to repentance and faith. In this sense the word "sacrament," meaning a mutual covenant pledge, becomes especially appropriate in connection with baptism. The candidate pledges love and loyalty to his/her Lord and Saviour, and God also makes an irrevocable pledge to the believer to do all that He must do to save that individual. God will never abrogate this pledge made in the baptismal covenant, for He loves with an everlasting love. Though the baptized one may fall from grace and reject salvation, God's pledge to save always remains. His love will follow and woo the one who may have fallen away until the very end,

[8]Bonhoeffer, *The Cost of Discipleship*, p. 45.
[9]Bacchiocchi, *Divine Rest for Human Restlessness*, p. 121.
[10]White, *Seventh-day Adventist Bible Commentary*, Vol. 6, pp. 1074–75.

until the fallen one has come back to faith or has utterly and completely turned away from the Father.

Finally, baptism signifies membership in the body of Christ, the church. But one does not join the church in the same way one joins Kiwanis or any other human institution. One is divinely plucked from one context and plunged into another—not without volition, of course, but God takes the initiative and acts to bring it about. The church is the new context into which God places the believer. The church is to receive, encourage, admonish, and nurture him/her in the faith. Baptism is thus a corporate as well as an individual event. Private baptism should never take place. The church, by its representatives, should always be present, because the baptized becomes a responsible church member and a part of the body of Christ.

To the church has been entrusted the responsibility of baptizing new believers, providing a visible demonstration of the covenant relationship between God and the believer. Can the church offer that which is so holy to anyone who is actually unbelieving, unconverted, and scornful, and still be true to its calling? Can grace be offered apart from the call to follow Christ? The answer should be obvious, for the church as a corporate entity also has the responsibility to guard the truth entrusted to it. For this reason baptism ought not be granted too readily in many cases, nor withheld too easily in others. Without evidence of conversion and transformation, baptism should not be administered at any age. The fundamental question posed to every candidate is not, "Do you understand and accept the teachings of the gospel?" but, "Have you died to sin and do you now live for Christ, to serve Him?" Indiscriminate baptism must cease, for, as Willimon says, "It is dishonest, if not downright cruel, to entice people with rosebuds, lace, sentiment, self-help [free Bibles and other religious knick-knacks], and end up tacking them on a cross."[11]

For those who have truly committed their lives to Christ, however, baptism is a deeply moving, solemnly joyous occasion. One of my former church members expressed this in a way that I will never forget. Suffering for some time with terminal cancer, Ruby had surrendered what was left of her life to Christ and requested baptism. She was extremely weak that day and was helped into the baptistry. It was right after being buried in baptism and rising to her new life in Christ that she became aware that the warm water buoyed her up. She could stand on her own with that support surrounding her, and she felt great! "I could stay here forever," she said. That's the idea! Surrounded,

[11]Willimon, *The Service of God*, p. 115 (insertion mine).

buoyed, by the love of Jesus we can stay with Him forever. Who would ever wish to leave?

Because baptism is such a significant event for the candidate and the church, because all the angels in heaven rejoice when one sinner repents and accepts Jesus as Saviour and Lord, the baptism must never be stuck in the worship service as an afterthought. The entire worship service must be planned around this event. Prayers, Scripture readings, sermon, hymns, and music must all focus on the baptism, providing the liturgical opportunity for the congregation to join the candidate, and the heavenly host, in celebration and in singing the new song of redemption and praise.

Lord's Supper

The narrative accounts of the first Lord's Supper are found in Matthew 26, Mark 14, Luke 22, and John 13. The passage used most frequently as the words of institution, read at communion services prior to the distribution, is 1 Cor 11:23–26. In order to get the full impact of Paul's words, we quote the passage in a wider context.

> In the following directives I have no praise for you, for your meetings do more harm than good. In the first place, I hear that when you come together as a church, there are divisions among you, and to some extent I believe it. No doubt there have to be differences among you to show which of you have God's approval. When you come together, it is not the Lord's Supper you eat, for as you eat, each of you goes ahead without waiting for anybody else. One remains hungry, another gets drunk. Don't you have homes to eat and drink in? Or do you despise the church of God and humiliate those who have nothing? What shall I say to you? Shall I praise you for this? Certainly not! For I received from the Lord what I also passed on to you: The Lord Jesus, on the night he was betrayed, took bread, and when he had given thanks, he broke it and said, "This is my body, which is for you; do this in remembrance of me." In the same way, after supper he took the cup, saying, "This cup is the new covenant in my blood; do this, whenever you drink it, in remembrance of me." For whenever you eat this bread and drink this cup, you proclaim the Lord's death until he comes. Therefore, whoever eats the bread or drinks the cup of the Lord in an unworthy manner will be guilty of sinning against the body and blood of the Lord. A man ought to examine himself before he eats of the bread and drinks of the cup. For anyone who eats and drinks without recognizing the body of the Lord eats and drinks judgment on himself. That is why many among you are weak and sick, and a number of you have fallen asleep. But if we judged ourselves, we would not come under judgment. When we are judged by the Lord, we are being disciplined

so that we will not be condemned with the world. So then, my brothers, when you come together to eat, wait for each other. If anyone is hungry, he should eat at home, so that when you meet together it may not result in judgment (1 Cor 11:17–34, NIV).

Three vital questions emerge from a study of this passage: (1) How are we to understand the presence of Christ in the Lord's Supper? (2) What is meant by "remembrance"? (3) How frequently should communion be celebrated?

Christ's Presence

The mode of Christ's presence in the Lord's Supper has been a divisive issue in Christianity for centuries. The issue still remains unresolved and contributes in no small way to disunity among Christians. Volumes have been written by theologians attempting to make a Catholic, a Lutheran, a Zwinglian, a Calvinist, or a Wesleyan out of the apostle Paul. Paul's statement in the passage above is often read through the spectacles of a particular theological tradition instead of permitting the apostle to speak for himself.

Paul wrote to a group of people struggling with the question of how to live as Christians in a pagan society. It is not surprising that pagan customs might cling to the new church. Feasting was common in which orgies of eating took place. The practice of eating together was carried over into the church and became known as love-feasts, the first Christian potlucks. Paul rebukes the Corinthian congregation for separating into cliques at such feasts, the rich eating with the rich and the poor with the poor. Often the poor had little or nothing to eat. Bitterness, envy, selfishness, and exclusiveness inevitably resulted. Sometimes the eating and drinking were excessive, so much so that Paul was moved to question, "Do you despise the church of God and humiliate those who have nothing?"

It is obvious the apostle was not dealing with a doctrinal issue, but with the practical issues of Christian living, Christian social behavior, and, ultimately, worship. He was not doing what theologians have since done with his words; he was not formulating a doctrine concerning the mode of Christ's presence in communion. He simply repeats the Lord's own words, saying, "This is my body," and, "This is the new covenant in my blood."

Certain words in the passage take on special importance in relation to the context: "do this" in connection with eating the bread; "do this as often as you drink it" in connection with drinking the cup; "for as often as you eat this bread and drink the cup you proclaim the Lord's death until he comes" (11:26, NAS). These references are all in connection with the *congregation's* participation in the communion service. The emphasis is not on the manner in which Christ is present, but on the manner in which believers are present.

The context of chapter 11 reveals what Paul is saying: that the same spirit of sacrifice and giving and sharing that Jesus demonstrated ought to characterize the life and worship of God's new people. Communion, for Paul, provides a unique opportunity for the realization and manifestation of the life of Christ to reveal itself in the fellowship of His people.[12] The problem, therefore, is not with the presence of Christ. Scripture simply says He is present! In harmony with Scripture, Ellen G. White makes no attempt to answer the question as to the mode of His presence. She simply bears witness to the fact that He is present. "Christ by the Holy Spirit is there to set the seal to His own ordinance. He is there to convict and soften the heart. . . . For the repentant, broken-hearted one He is waiting. All things are ready for that soul's reception. He who washed the feet of Judas longs to wash every heart from the stains of sin."[13]

The problem is not with Christ's presence in communion, but with *our* presence. Paul's emphasis is on the practice of communion, on the presence corporately of the body of Christ—the church—, on every member sharing in that worship experience and then being the church in the world. The command of Jesus to "do this," to regularly celebrate communion, is not satisfied by an administrative decision to have communion on a given Sabbath. It is satisfied when *you* and *I* are present, really present in mind, body, and soul, and in faith eager to share the spiritual blessings of giving and receiving and sharing. Paul is not saying, "You had better believe this about communion!" He is saying, "You had better do this about communion!" To believe the right things about communion and not do them constitutes denial. When we are absent from communion we are saying loudly and clearly, "I really don't believe what God's Word says about communion."

Our presence is as important as the Lord's presence. If we are not both present there is no communion. We must be present spiritually, symbolically, and physically. Our real presence at communion symbolizes our faith and trust in the Saviour. It is our physical confession that we recognize ourselves as sinners in need of cleansing and divine grace every day. It is our acknowledgement that we participate in the

[12]This is true also in relation to footwashing as a part of communion. Footwashing is discussed in chapter 9 as an example of how SDA theology can be dramatized in SDA liturgy.

[13]White, *Desire of Ages*, p. 656.

great controversy between good and evil that rages in the inner being as well as in the cosmos. Our presence at the Lord's Supper proclaims that we are really present in faith and in surrender to the lordship of Christ. Change does not occur in the bread and wine, but in those worshipers who receive Christ by faith.

Communion provides the liturgical opportunity to demonstrate this surrender, the body of Christ offering itself anew in faith and in obedient service and discipleship. This is particularly dramatized in the prayer over the bread and the cup and in the public reading of the words of institution. It is the church that needs consecration, for it is the people of God who are the true sacrament: broken bread and poured-out wine for a world in desperate need of a Saviour and the righteousness of God.

Instead of St. John Chrysostom's eucharistic prayers, "Make this bread the precious body of your Christ," and, "Make that which is in the chalice the precious blood of your Christ," we should pray, before eating and drinking, "Make this church to be as the broken body and the shed blood of your Son for the sake of the world." What is it that is being offered in communion: bread and wine for the church, or the church for Christ and the world? Perhaps we need to recover the practice of the early church and present the bread and wine to be used in the service as offerings to God, signifying the offering of the church to righteousness and service. To eat this bread and drink this wine is to internalize the offering, the surrender.

The words of institution have no effect on the elements of bread and wine, but they should have great effect on the church. It is the church that needs to hear the words from the Word so that it can respond and become what it has eaten, what it confesses to be. The real presence of Christ is not identified with the elements, but with the gathered body of believers.

Communion also provides the church with a window on the world. It sees things far differently when in union with Christ and with fellow believers, on its knees in humility to wash feet and then eat a meager meal of bread and wine. One cannot do this and be oblivious to what it means to be the church in the world. Such a simple meal excludes no one. All are equals at the table of the Lord. All are beggars. It is the body of Christ that is being nurtured and strengthened for service and victory and holiness. "We become what we eat" is as true spiritually as it is physically. The church is first the body gathered at the table of the Lord—always coming together to share Christ, to feed on Him, to acknowledge Him, to worship and praise Him, to hear, to obey, and to remember Him. Because of this unity of believers and

Christ, to despise brothers and sisters in the church while eating the bread and drinking the wine of the Lord's Supper, as the Corinthians were doing, is to negate the very meaning of the service and to despise Christ Himself, the Head of the body.

We do not believe Christ is locally present in the elements, but that He is present by His Spirit in the church, and therefore in the church's celebration of communion, to impart His grace and the benefits of His death, resurrection, and ministry in heaven to all who believe and receive. Jesus said: "I am the bread of life. He who comes to me will never go hungry, and he who believes in me will never be thirsty. . . . For my Father's will is that everyone who looks to the Son and believes in him shall have eternal life, and I will raise him up at the last day. . . . Just as the living Father sent me and I live because of the Father, so the one who feeds on me will live because of me. This is the bread that came down from heaven" (John 6:35, 40, 57–58, NIV).

Can the Christian commune with the Lord and with fellow believers in the beautiful service of the Lord's Supper and remain the same as when he/she entered the sanctuary?

Remembrance

Jesus said, "Do this in remembrance of me." What exactly did He mean? Was it His intention that in our celebration of the Lord's Supper we focus our thoughts only on the past, on Calvary? Or did he have a fuller perspective in mind? The Adventist understanding of atonement suggests the latter, and Jesus' statement, together with the context of 1 Corinthians 11, appears to support such a wider perspective.

The Greek term translated "remembrance" is *anamnesis*. In classical Greek the term meant much more than a mere memorializing in terms of bringing to mind a past event. It evokes an expanding of memory encompassing a completion, a finishing, rather than a single event. It conveys the sense of a memoir, the story of a total life and a finished work. Jesus said we are to eat the bread and drink the cup in remembrance of *Him*—not just in memory of His suffering and death but in remembrance of the total ministry of the Saviour. Communion is not like placing a wreath on the tomb of the unknown soldier once a year, but is rather a calling to mind of the full gospel repeatedly.

Anamnesis, therefore, means a calling to mind of the Christ who is portrayed in the book of Hebrews as ascended High Priest, pleading the cause of sinners for whom He died, and of the Christ portrayed in the book of Revelation as both the Lamb of Calvary and the triumphant and returning Judge and Vindicator of God and redeemed mankind.

What is remembered by the communicant is not the crucifixion, but the crucified, ascended, reigning, and victorious Lord of Lords.

There is far greater danger to the meaning and celebration of the Lord's Supper in a narrow, limited *anamnesis* than in some of the unfounded fears we may have of an emphasis on eucharistic worship and devotion. Perhaps those who would criticize eucharistic worship ought to analyze the source of their dissatisfaction. What is it they dislike about it? Do they disbelieve in the reality of, and necessity for, Christ's atoning ministry, which has shifted to the heavenly sanctuary preparatory to His return? Is it that they, while appreciating that He has gone to prepare a place for them, dislike the idea that they must be prepared for that place by means of the inner ministry of the Holy Spirit? The Lord's Supper is not a memorial to a dead Christ, but a memoir of the living Lord who is actively engaged, from the heavenly courts, in a sanctifying ministry through the Holy Spirit. To truly celebrate the Lord's Supper is to recall and accept His contemporary ministry as well as His willingness to bear the cross. "Therefore he is able to save completely those who come to God through him, because he always lives to intercede for them. Such a High Priest meets our need—one who is holy, blameless, pure, set apart for sinners, exalted above the heavens" (Heb 7:25, NIV). The work of Calvary is not yet completed—it is only finished in that He who died once for our sin will never die again. It is even now in the final stages of that completion at God's right hand, and then He will return. Thus in the *anamnesis* can be found all the past, present, and future of the atonement.

The pure memorialist excludes the living Christ as High Priest, for memory alone reaches only into the past. To truly remember Christ in communion is to reach up with faith into the sanctuary above and into the future with confident and unparalleled hope. The pure memorialist actually believes in the absence of Christ, whereas the all-encompassing memory believes in His presence both in the sanctuary above and in His body—the church—by His Spirit. The sacrament is not just a memorial of a past event, but is in fact a dramatic portrayal and proclamation of Christ's sacrifice still pleaded in heaven before the Father. Thus the bread we eat symbolizes both the broken body of Christ on the cross and the scarred Christ who pleads with God on our behalf. The wine we drink symbolizes the blood He shed on the cross and that He took into the heavenly sanctuary.

Neither Luther, Calvin, nor John Wesley were pure memorialists. That distinction belongs to Ulrich Zwingli of Zurich. John and Charles Wesley wrote some of the most profound eucharistic hymns—166 to be exact—which move in thought from Calvary to Christ's work as High

Priest and His second advent. Following are the texts for three of them:[14]

100

1 Returning to His throne above, The Friend of sinners cried,
DO THIS in memory of My love: He spoke the word, and died.

2 He tasted death for everyone: The Saviour of mankind
Out of our sight to heaven is gone, But left His pledge behind.

3 His sacramental pledge we take, Nor will we let it go;
Till in the clouds our Lord comes back, We thus His death will show.

4 Come quickly, Lord, for whom we mourn, and comfort all that grieve;
Prepare the bride, and then return, And to Thyself receive.

5 Now to Thy glorious kingdom come; Thou hast a token given;
And while Thy arms receive us home, Recall Thy pledge in heaven.

116

1 Victim Divine, Thy grace we claim, While thus Thy precious death we show;
Once offer'd up, a spotless Lamb, In Thy great temple here below,
Thou didst for all mankind atone, And standest now before the throne.

2 Thou standest in the holiest place, As now for guilty sinners slain;
Thy blood of sprinkling speaks, and prays, All-prevalent for helpless man;
Thy blood is still our ransom found, And spreads salvation all around.

3 The smoke of Thy atonement here, Darken'd the sun and rent the veil,
Made the new way to heaven appear, And show'd the great Invisible;
Well pleased in Thee our God look'd down, And called His rebels to a crown.

4 He still respects Thy sacrifice, Its savour sweet doth always please;
The offering smokes through earth and skies, Diffusing life, and joy, and peace;
To these Thy lower courts it comes, And fills them with divine perfumes.

5 We need not now go up to heaven, To bring the long-sought Saviour down;

[14]From "Hymns on the Lord's Supper" by John and Charles Wesley, in J. Ernest Rattenbury, *The Eucharistic Hymns of John and Charles Wesley* (London: Epworth Press, 1948), pp. 195–249.

Thou art to all already given, Thou dost even now Thy banquet crown:
To every faithful soul appear, And show Thy real presence here.

118

1 Live, our Eternal Priest, By men and angels blest!
Jesus Christ the Crucified, He who did for us atone,
From the cross where once He died, Now He up to heaven is gone.

2 He ever lives, and prays For all the faithful race;
In the holiest place above, Sinners' advocate He stands,
Pleads for us His dying love, Shows for us His bleeding hands.

3 His body torn and rent, He doth to God present,
In that dear memorial shows, Israel's chosen tribes imprest;
All our names the Father knows, Reads them on our Aaron's breast.

4 He reads, while we beneath Present our Saviour's death,
Do as Jesus bids us do, Signify His flesh and blood,
Him in a memorial show, Offer up the Lamb to God.

5 From this thrice hallowed shade, Which Jesus' cross hath made,
Image of His sacrifice, Never, never will we move,
Till with all His saints we rise, Rise, and take our place above.[15]

Calvary is not repeatable, but in the broken bread and poured-out wine of the eucharist we participate in the memoir, looking back, looking up, and looking forward to a bright future for God's people. We need to remember the whole story. Communion is a dramatic narration in ritual form of the whole *kerygma*, the whole story of redemption. Jesus died once, but His intercession and High Priestly ministry are perpetual until probation ends. He redeems once, He delivers continuously. The sacrament signifies what He did for us, what He is doing for us, and what He will do for us.

Adventist communion is no simple memorial—it is a revealed awareness of God's purpose in creation, redemption, and ultimate fulfillment. Adventist celebration of the Lord's Supper ought to throb with delicious anticipation of the heavenly feast soon to be shared by the saints in glory. The sacrament is a pledge, a promise, of that triumphant event still to come. Triumphant joy is the emotion eucharistic celebration ought to release.

[15]In *The Church Hymnal* published in 1941 by the Seventh-day Adventist Church, there are only six communion hymns, one of which focuses on footwashing. None of them is by the Wesleys. We can only hope that the new hymnal to be released in 1985 will contain more communion hymns.

Communion is more than memorial for the Adventist, for he/she knows that at the very moment of communion Christ is presenting His sacrifice before the Father. It is a perpetual offering, a pleading of His blood, until the work of the heavenly tribunal is finished and the Saviour prepares for His triumphant return to execute the final judgment of the tribunal.

Ellen White comments that "as faith contemplates our Lord's great sacrifice, the soul assimilates the spiritual life of Christ."[16] Thus for her communion is more than mere memorial. In contemplation of the external elements of bread and wine the liturgical drama produces an inward experience of Christ. She also said: "The communion service points to Christ's second coming. . . . These are the things we are never to forget. The love of Jesus with its constraining power, is to be kept fresh in our memory. Christ has instituted this service so that it may speak to our senses of the love of God that has been expressed in our behalf. . . . It is only because of His death that we can look with joy to His second coming. His sacrifice is the center of our hope. Upon this we must fix our faith."[17] This is an inclusive statement. In her mind what is remembered in communion is not only Christ's death but also His return.

It is not the church that offers the sacrifice of Christ, but Christ Himself who became obedient to death and is now engaged in the completion of His atoning sacrifice in heaven. Though resurrected and glorified, it is with nail-pierced hands and feet and thorn-scarred brow that He stands as our Advocate before the Father. This the church remembers in communion as, made up of baptized members who have faith in Him, it offers itself to be what God has ordained it to be: His instrument for world evangelization, willing to suffer as He suffered in the finishing of that mission. Perhaps the following should be read at Adventist communion services:

> Your attitude should be the same as that of Christ Jesus: Who, being in very nature God, did not consider equality with God something to be grasped, but made himself nothing, taking the very nature of a servant, being made in human likeness. And being found in appearance as a man, he humbled himself and became obedient to death—even death on a cross! Therefore God exalted him to the highest place and gave him the name that is above every name, that at the name of Jesus every knee should bow, in heaven and on the earth and under the earth, and every tongue confess that Jesus Christ is Lord, to the glory of God the Father (Phil 2:5–11, NIV).

[16]White, *Desire of Ages*, p. 661.
[17]Ibid., p. 660.

The Christ we remember when we commune is He who is continuing to serve His church and offer Himself as intercessor for the saints. It would appear, therefore, that Adventists, who have unique insight into His ministry in heaven, should have an exceedingly high regard for the Lord's Supper and celebrate it often. The communicant ought to come away from the table filled with new resolve to strive for the reunion in history of the fragmented body of Christ. This should add new zeal to the mission of the Seventh-day Adventist Church as it calls God's people to a visible unity based on Scripture in preparation for the Lord's return.

Just as the Sabbath prefigures the return of Christ, so also does the celebration of the Lord's Supper. In its gathering around the table of the Lord the church prefigures in anticipation the gathering on Mount Zion with the Lamb of God in her midst on that great day. A consecrated church becomes a conscientious church. From its worship its mission emerges and into the world it goes as Christ's body.

Frequency

Jesus said, "Do this, as often as you drink it, in remembrance of me." Then Paul adds, "For as often as you eat this bread and drink the cup, you proclaim the Lord's death until He comes" (1 Cor 11:25–26, NAS). These verses seem to assume a frequent celebration of the Lord's Supper, and declare that such celebration has a contemporary proclamatory function based on Calvary and focused on the future.

In many denominations, including our own, it has become virtually a set tradition to conduct communion services four times each year. Perhaps at the outset of our discussion we should keep in mind our Lord's words: "They worship me in vain; their teachings are but rules taught by men. You have let go of the commands of God and are holding on to the traditions of men. . . . Thus you nullify the word of God by your tradition that you have handed down" (Mark 7:7–8, 13, NIV). This poses the question: Are we bound by tradition to four celebrations a year?

Scripture seems to indicate that communion was a frequent event in the worship of the New Testament converts (Acts 2:42–47; 1 Cor 11). And ample evidence exists indicating that the early church immediately following the New Testament period celebrated communion weekly and the believers partook weekly. Worship normally consisted of the proclamation of the Word and the Lord's Supper. During the sixteenth century attempt to restore apostolic Christianity, both Luther and Calvin advocated weekly communion. It was Ulrich Zwingli who did not consider communion an important part of Christian celebration and limited it to four times each year: at Easter, Pentecost, in the fall, and at Christmas. It was Zwingli who tragically separated the Lord's Supper from the Lord's Day. During the Reformation, Protestant worship services became decidedly didactic in nature, and the result was an impoverishment of worship life. Man's whole being was not being addressed and fed in worship. The appeal was more to the mind than to all the senses.

John Calvin did not want to replace sacramental worship with a preaching service. He wanted to restore the Lord's Supper to its New Testament simplicity and at the same time give Scripture and preaching their proper place. His liturgy, divided like that of the early church into the liturgy of the Word and the liturgy of the Upper Room, included a confession of sin, a prayer for pardon, and the recitation of the Apostles' Creed. He introduced the recitation of the Ten Commandments in meter, with the two tables separated by a short prayer for God's grace to keep His law.

It was not Calvin but the civil magistrates in Geneva who were responsible for the separation of the Lord's Supper from the regular weekly worship in that city, overruling the spiritual leader of the Genevan congregations. Calvin wrote in response: "It was ordained to be frequently used among all Christians in order that they might frequently return in memory to Christ's passion, by such remembrance to sustain and strengthen their faith, and urge themselves to sing thanksgiving to God and to proclaim His goodness; finally, by it to nourish mutual love and among themselves to give witness to this love, and discern its bond in the unity of Christ's body." Also: " . . . this custom which enjoins us to take communion once a year is a veritable invention of the devil. . . . the Lord's table should have been spread at least once a week for the assembly of christians, and the promises declared in it should feed us spiritually. . . . all, like hungry men, should flock to such a bounteous repast."[18]

When it comes to John Wesley it is interesting to note that the Lord's Supper took on deeper meaning for him following his conversion in 1738. All his remaining life he was an itinerant evangelist; nevertheless his appreciation for sacramental worship increased. He needed the sacrament as spiritual nourishment, together with daily Bible reading, to sustain his new life in Christ. His writings reveal that he never changed his attitude about the importance of communion and its frequent celebration. Diaries for the last eight years of his life testify to his

[18]*Institutes of the Christian Religion*, Book 4, ed. John T. McNeill and trans. Ford Lewis Battles (Philadelphia: Westminster Press, 1960), chap. 17, par. 44 and 46.

practice of communing each Sunday and often on Saturday evenings as well. Between 1785 and 1790 he communed once every other day, and between 1787 and 1791 he missed Sunday communion only once due to sickness. It was as a direct result of the Wesleyan revival, decidedly evangelistic and pietistic in nature, that large crowds began to attend the communion services in the Anglican parishes prior to the formation of the Methodist Church after Wesley's death. This revival offers a startling example of the place communion had in a life of sincere and deep religious piety and devotion. Such is the power that faithful preaching of the Word has on the worship life of a spiritually awakened people. Some communion services were four to five hours long in order to accommodate the crowds. What an evangelistic methodology!

Unfortunately, in American Methodism Wesley's sacramental appreciation was buried under the image of him as evangelist and revivalist, under his stress on personal religion, assurance of forgiveness, and holiness of life. In fact, however, John Wesley was both an evangelist and sacramentalist—a truly balanced preacher and churchman.

When, finally, in 1785 Wesley ordained three men for ministry in America, the act was precipitated by the shortage of ordained ministers with ecclesiastical authority to celebrate the Lord's Supper. Because Anglican clergy were beginning to refuse communion to Methodists, Wesley was moved to take upon himself the responsibility. At that moment of decision the Methodist movement became a church.

Still, because he was an evangelist at heart, Wesley saw converting power in the sacrament. That is precisely why he encouraged weekly communion and welcomed all who wished to participate. He linked the evangelistic preaching of the Word with the celebration of the Lord's Supper, one of his major contributions to modern Christianity. This linkage demonstrated a wholistic approach in meeting the spiritual needs of persons. Of this accomplishment Raymond Billington says: "His recovery of the twin pillars of the liturgy—Word and Eucharist, Evangelism and Sacramentalism—was a truly prophetic act."[19]

Wesley prepared a liturgy for Methodist congregations which was not widely used by Methodist ministers in America. For over 100 years they prepared their own liturgies with little reference to Wesley's views. The revivalistic influence in early American life caused preaching to dominate worship services. Not until 1905 was an order of service reintroduced to the Methodist hymnal. Thus communion in

[19]Raymond J. Billington, *The Liturgical Movement in Methodism* (London: Epworth Press, 1969), p. 128.

contemporary Methodism has a more prominent place than it did in the nineteenth century, at the time Ellen G. White became a Methodist and later spearheaded the Advent movement.

Adventism thus inherited the early American approach to communion, greatly influenced by Zwingli and revivalism rather than by Wesley himself. But Ellen White herself urges a far different practice. At the time she wrote, both Methodists and Adventists were holding communion services four times yearly, and she said, "Washing feet and the Lord's Supper should be more frequently practiced by us."[20] She is careful not to say how frequently, thus leaving the matter open for congregations and pastors to decide, but it is obvious she was not satisfied with communion celebrations only four times yearly.

When the question of frequency of communion is raised, a number of objections are made which require attention.

It is objected that more emphasis on the Lord's Supper would be a departure from Adventist heritage. But what, exactly, is the Adventist heritage with respect to frequency of communion? Is it Zwinglianism? Is it American Methodism as opposed to Wesleyanism? Is it revivalism? Or is it New Testament and apostolic practice? Perhaps we ought to trace our spiritual tap root back into the New Testament period rather than follow tangential offshoots.

It is objected that the gospel is proclaimed in the ministry of the Word, therefore communion is a non-essential, at best a bothersome thing, an event to be avoided, a day to go church visiting. But the Word says that the Lord's Supper proclaims Christ's death until He comes again. In such a visually oriented age as ours, it was never so true that the liturgical drama of communion is proclamatory. In fact no other act of the church so effectively dramatizes and proclaims the entire gospel: creation (bread and wine), incarnation (the presence of Christ), atonement (body broken and blood shed), resurrection (communion with the risen Christ), exaltation (praise and worship of the Lord of Lords), and eschatology (His promise to return). In few sermons are all these gospel truths simultaneously declared. Only the communion liturgy lifts these saving truths above the human failure to believe them, proclaim them, and dramatize them adequately.

A parishioner once said to me, "I forget what is said in church, but I never forget what is done in church." In the Lord's Supper liturgy, the gospel appeal is to the human senses of sight and taste as well as hearing. The modern generation's perception of reality has been influenced by television. Today's post-literate generation perceives reality

[20]Manuscript Release No. 347, p. 23.

through the immediacy of direct experience. This has tremendous implications for Christian worship. Our children today do not ask about worship, "What did the preacher say?"—they ask, "What happened?"

The increasing importance and power of the dramatic and the visual for the late twentieth century is succinctly pointed out by David Watson:

> The spoken or written word by itself makes less and less impact on our modern society. All the communicators of today have to be influenced by the essential nature of television, or else they fail entirely to communicate with any but a tiny section of society.
>
> This is a vital fact that the church has been tragically slow to realise, or at least to accept. Most churches rely heavily on the spoken or written word for communication, and then wonder why so few people find the Christian faith to be relevant. The truth is that we live in a world that is almost dominated by drama, and it is only when the church comes to terms with this in any serious and realistic way that it will be able to speak in the 'language' of today. If it fails to do this, any effective heralding of God's word will be severely handicapped. The church, in the eyes of the world, will be limping slowly along, supported on the crutches of past methods, and quite unable to keep up with the rapidly increasing speed of change within our culture. . . .
>
> I wonder, however, how often the congregation leaves a service with the feeling that it has just experienced 'unforgettable communication'? Having witnessed something of the potential of mime and drama, not to mention music and dance, when it comes to effective communication both within and without a church building, I am convinced of the need to explore prayerfully and sensitively other forms of presentation in addition to the conventional sermon from the pulpit. Nothing can or should replace the straight proclamation of God's word, but there is much that can illustrate it most effectively. Mistakes will no doubt be made, but the alternative is to cling fiercely to traditional forms for fear of making a mistake—and that is a mistake in itself! Given the necessary context of much prayer and love, the determination to be true to the Scriptures, the desire to glorify Christ, and the willingness to give and receive correction when necessary, there is much that can be done to make the church's communication of the gospel far more powerful than it is at present. As with other issues, the children of this world are so often wiser than the children of light.

The visual, dramatic service of communion can be one of the most powerful means of communicating the gospel, speaking to this generation as no sermon can.

[21]David Watson, *I Believe in the Church* (Grand Rapids, Mich.: Eerdmans, 1978), pp. 221, 223.

Some object that frequent celebration of the Lord's Supper creates logistical problems, especially with respect to footwashing in large congregations. There are bad and good problems. This is a good problem. Praise God if so many people attend communion that it causes logistical problems! We need not be so time-conscious that we resent a little extra time spent in a major spiritual event. It is unthinkable for the Christian church to succumb to this kind of pressure from the generation that will spend five or six hours a day in front of the TV. What better use could we make of our time than to spend it in communion with our Lord?

Some also object that frequent communion is destructive of meaning and reverence and becomes mere repetition. We need only quote Jesus: "Do this"! For the truly converted Christian, reverence and meaning ought to increase with frequency, not decrease. One is moved to inquire: If meaning and reverence are preserved by infrequent communion, how is it that so many Seventh-day Adventists, who come to hear preaching regularly, absent themselves from communion? Has it become so holy they prefer to omit it altogether from the devotional life?

Individuals have been heard to say, "I don't get anything out of communion." That is no reason for a Christian not to partake. If one receives nothing, it is not the fault of the sacrament or the number of times it is celebrated. Four times a year only provides fewer opportunities to get nothing out of it. But the Lord established it for our spiritual benefit and commanded its frequent celebration—that should be enough for His people. If a person loses interest in communion, is repetition to blame? Or does the problem lie elsewhere? We do not get bored with eating three meals a day; hunger returns regularly and insistently, prompting us to eat again. And there are other human hungers that demand immediate and repetitive satisfaction. Frequent communion likewise satisfies the spiritual hunger of the believer. There is no such thing as a boring communion service. There are only bored people. Jesus said, "Blessed are those who hunger and thirst for righteousness, for they will be filled" (Matt 5:6, NIV). The desire to commune, the hungering and thirsting that communion satisfies, is related to the new life in Christ and the desire for spiritual growth and sanctification. The Holy Spirit that abides in the believer yearns for communion with the Father and the Son and moves the believer to the celebration of the Lord's Supper. Frequent communion strengthens our commitment and deepens our relationship with our Lord.

Another objection raised to communion as a regular part of the worship service is that set ritual inhibits freedom and spontaneity. But are we prepared to accept unrestrained, and at times offensive and boorish, emotion and enthusiasm instead? It may be dangerous to impose upon the church a form of worship developed in another era and another culture, but it is equally as dangerous to have no form at all, for that can let loose all sorts of "spirits" counterproductive to worship in Spirit and in truth. It is true that Ellen White says both baptism and the Lord's Supper "are regarded too much as a form." But in the same passage she says of them: "They were instituted for a purpose. Our senses need to be quickened to lay hold of the mystery of godliness."[21] The sacraments should not be *regarded* as forms; they should not be thought of in that way. If we do so we will miss their intent entirely. Yet the very repetition of the acts of communion increases their significance. Willimon remarks that "the normality, the constancy of the eucharist is part of its power."[22] It takes a Christian lifetime to develop Christlike character. Sanctification is a process from which one does not graduate, and frequent, repeated participation in the Lord's Supper is as much a part of that process as willingness to hear and do the Word of God.

No two sermons are alike, but the essential liturgical elements of communion are always the same. They cannot be changed or the result will no longer be Christian communion. Surrounding liturgical details may be changed, but not those of the communion itself. It was meant to be that way: a repetitive, habitual, common event made up of the offering of bread and wine, the recitation of the words of institution, the prayers of consecration, the breaking of the bread, and the distribution. The communion drama is to the point and concrete. In it the kingdom takes on visible form. Its meaning is unmistakable. There is stability in the unchangeableness and sameness of communion. It is disciplinary and suggests permanence. To alter these liturgical elements when communing parishioners who are in extreme illness is immediately threatening, and produces insecurity. Communion simply cannot be celebrated without repetition, and that is good, not bad. Ellen G. White says, "The truest humility is to receive with thankful heart any provision made on our behalf,"[23] and, we might add, as often as possible.

Mrs. White is in harmony with Wesley's view that the Lord's Supper has converting influence in that she indicates that all who wish should be allowed to partake even though they, like Judas, lack faith.

[21]White, *Desire of Ages*, p. 660.
[22]Willimon, *The Service of God*, p. 127.
[23]White, *Desire of Ages*, p. 646.

It is an "inducement for the sinner to receive Him, to repent, and to be cleansed from the defilement of sin."[24] The Lord's Supper has, therefore, both a converting and confirming power.

One final word needs to be said. The above is not a plea for the elaboration of the communion rite. On the contrary, simplification is required. In the preparatory liturgy to eating the bread and drinking the cup, it is best to use only the words of institution from 1 Cor 11:23–26. Let these words speak according to their simple meaning, with no attempt at liturgical extravagance or theological web-weaving. That is the best way to preserve the meaning of the Lord's Supper as thanksgiving, sacrifice, mystery, and memoir. In fact the Lord's Supper defies a complete and definitive explanation. What is needed is simply to commune, and often.

There are ways, however, to highlight the meaning and significance of communion without detraction, and in ways that meet sensory needs. For example this could very effectively be done by the use of sanctuary lighting. The footwashing service should have a somber mood of sorrow for sin and repentance. This mood could be dramatized and created by lowering the sanctuary lights with one or two soft candles burning on the communion table during the footwashing. The lights in the rooms where the rite takes place should also be low with some candles in strategic places. While the congregation is washing feet the sanctuary lights could be turned up to full brilliance, the candles extinguished and removed, and bright spotlights beamed on the communion table with its pure white linen. The mood of the members as they return from footwashing will immediately shift from the somberness of repentance and confession to the brightness and brilliance of new life and hope in the message of forgiveness and resurrection. The senses will respond and thrilled voices be raised to sing the new song, joining the angelic throng of the heavenly sanctuary in praise to the Father and the Son.

Discussion Questions

1. Should evangelists baptize? If so, under what conditions? If not, who should and when?
2. Why do you think some members of the SDA Church absent themselves from the Lord's Supper? What can be done to resolve this problem?

[24]White, *Desire of Ages*, p. 655.

3. What creative ways can you think of to liturgically dramatize the meaning of baptism and the Lord's Supper?
4. Is there merit in solving the logistical problem with respect to communion by having the footwashing on Friday evening and the communion proper on Sabbath morning?

Adventist Worship Illustrates Adventist Beliefs

Part Three

Worship and the Order of Service / 8

Two things were said by Norval Pease in *And Worship Him* which have been foundational to our discussion in these chapters. He said worship cannot take place without liturgy, and that this liturgy should reflect theological beliefs. It is in the order of service that theology and liturgy meet. There everything we have been discussing is put together. The worship service is not a matter of indifference or of whim and fancy. In the order of service, theology and liturgy will either harmonize or clash. In this regard the minister's responsibility as worship leader is very great. That responsibility is reflected in Ellen G. White's statement: "Nothing that is sacred, nothing that pertains to the worship of God, should be treated with carelessness or indifference."[1]

Protestant worship cannot take place without the presence of the gathered congregation. This gathering implies much more than a group of people meeting together to worship. It implies the last-day unity of God's people, because God's last message begins with a call to worship Him as a united body of believers. Most descriptive of the worship of the last-day church is this statement from the Gospel of John: " . . . that He might also gather into one the children of God who are scattered abroad" (John 11:52). The worship of the last-day church should reflect its unity of belief and should give liturgical expression to that unity. Therefore it is important that the three distinguishing doctrines of the Seventh-day Adventist Church—Christ's Sabbath, heavenly ministry, and second advent—be liturgically illustrated in its worship services. These are the doctrines that will bring about the final unity of God's people. Therefore worship is not simply a collection of

[1]White, *Testimonies for the Church*, Vol. 5, p. 491.

congregations around the world, all worshiping and confessing Jesus as Lord (the ecumenical formula); worship is His people gathering together under His *lordship* in a unity of belief, set apart and identified as His true body.

Worship Requires Planning

If worship is this, then it requires careful planning as well as a careful educating of the congregation as to the meaning and significance of worship for the last-day church. Franklin Segler writes: "One of the explanations for much ineffective worship in our churches is the lack of serious planning on the part of leaders. This carelessness in planning may be due to the following facts: some leaders in worship have closed minds on the subject; their knowledge of the dynamics of participation may be limited; their poor theologizing about worship sets it apart as being irrelevant."[2] To think of corporate worship in nonliturgical terms is an exercise in futility. It is an attempt to avoid reality, the reality of living within the bounds of space and time. In any gathering of people there is an organization within space that occupies time. Worship is affected by our physical, earthly existence. It will have a form, therefore, whether that form is constructed ahead of time or is allowed to emerge out of group dynamics. But what form will it have? Shall we be content with chaos, with mediocrity, with ambiguity? Shall the corporate worship of the last-day church, designed to communicate important truths for the end times, be allowed to degenerate into unorganized hodge-podge and whimsical notions? Ellen White affirms that "His service should be made interesting and attractive and not be allowed to degenerate into a dry form."[3] However, form itself does not constitute dryness and degeneration. Worship degenerates *into* dry formalism when it is not made interesting and attractive by the worship leader and the participating congregation.

The minute we think of gathering, of singing, of praying, of communing, of preaching and listening, we must think about order. "God is not a God of confusion," says Paul, "but of peace, as in all the churches of the saints" (1 Cor 14:33). Furthermore, "Let all things be done properly and in an orderly manner" (1 Cor 14:40). To organize the activity of a worshiping group, no matter how slight or simple that organizing might be, means to engage in liturgical planning. The manner in which the gathering takes place and how it conducts its business

[2]Franklin Segler, *Christian Worship: Its Theology and Practice* (Nashville: Broadman Press, 1967), p. 185.

[3]White, *Testimonies for the Church*, Vol. 5, p. 609.

are determined by the confrontation implied in gathering, singing, praying, preaching, and communing.

The events of the end time are not necessarily chaotic or ambiguous. The worship of the last-day church should reflect an orderly progression toward a predetermined goal. The Holy Spirit has nothing in common with disorder and confusion. The whole end-time message exudes progression and order. There may be some disruptions because of man's activities, but from God's perspective all is in order. Events will occur according to plan and on time. Which shall the worship of the last-day church reflect: the orderliness and progression of the Creator, or the disruption and confusion of uncertain mankind?

Out of the dissolution of the old order, the old world, there will come a new order, a new world. That event ought also to be reflected in the orderly, organized solemnity of the worship of the last-day church. It would seem that the gifts of the Spirit for the end times would bring about an orderliness in keeping with God's own character. The worship of the last-day church, therefore, should be well ordered and edifying.

Criteria for Liturgical Form

If we are not to have "excessive liturgy," as Pease rightly warns, what should be the criteria for at least minimum form? Obviously for Seventh-day Adventists the first criteria must be the communication of the Word of God. This means that the entire worship service, not just the preaching of a sermon, should be considered a proclamatory event. Second, the structure of the service should provide the opportunity for emphasizing the major doctrines we hold: the Sabbath, the heavenly ministry of Christ, and His second advent, in particular. Third, the sacraments should be celebrated in such a way that room be provided, at least quarterly, in the main services of the church for the celebration of the Lord's Supper and baptism. When baptism and communion are celebrated they should provide the central focus of the worship hour and not be mere additions. That is to say, the focus of the entire worship service should be on the sacramental event. Hymns, Scripture reading, special music, sermon, prayers, should all be in harmony with the event being celebrated. The solemnity of worship is marred when an occasional event such as communion, baptism, child dedication, the ordination of elders and deacons, or even the installation of Sabbath School teachers, is simply stuck in somewhere in the service, having no liturgical relationship to the rest of the worship events.

While these elements—proclamation, doctrinal statement, and sacraments—should constitute the minimum form, they still leave plenty of room for many possibilities. Creativity and innovation and spontaneity are not excluded thereby. Our criteria for worship are based on the Word of God and our theological understanding of Word and worship. The Word helps us understand what should or should not be included in worship. We ought to capitalize on that which the Word indicates should be a part of the worship of the last-day church. At the same time it needs to be made clear that anything not consistent with the gospel of Christ and/or with Adventist thought must be excluded from Adventist worship. In this connection Peter Brunner says, "Words are the dominant element on which the form of worship is constructed. These words dare state nothing that contradicts the Gospel of Jesus Christ attested in Holy Writ. The demand must be made the more insistently, the more clearly we note that also the congregation's response to the Word proclaimed to it presents an indirect form of the Word's proclamation. The indissoluble interrelation of the sacramental and the sacrificial acts in worship demands that every word uttered in the course of worship remain under the jurisdiction of the prophetic and apostolic testimony of Scripture."[4]

The planning of the order of service takes place in the wide area that exists between what Peter Brunner calls the "absolutely commanded" and the "absolutely forbidden." In that area the church has wide latitude, but it is always a freedom exercised within the restraint imposed by the Holy Spirit and the written Word. Within that area we exercise our responsibility as representatives of the last-day message to church and world. Our ecumenical perspective and understanding indicate that in preparation for the return of Christ there is to be a "new" and united group of people, that a new name has been given to these people under which they are to assemble as the people of God (Rev 14:12), that their historic message of salvation in Christ is rooted in the Sabbath, Christ's heavenly ministry, and His coming again, and that the worship celebration of this expectant church is to be reflective of those elements. A certain timelessness of divine truth is to be reflected in the worship of the last-day church. Yet the last-day church must be keenly aware of the times and stand ready and willing to respond to mankind's searchings by casting eternal truth in contemporary language. This is particularly necessary in different cultural settings. Timeless truths must always be spoken to the times.

If the content of our worship form is substantive, timeless, and timely, as well as biblically historical, it should be considered to have an enduring faithfulness. The worship of the last-day church ought to

[4]Brunner, *Worship in the Name of Jesus*, p. 227.

bear the imprint of its Lord, its soon-coming Head, until the time He appears in the midst of His gathered people on Mount Zion. If, as we believe, the Seventh-day Adventist Church is the true ecumenical movement calling God's people to a unity based on Scripture, then the form of its worship ought to reflect that reality. The unifying character of our worship must rest firmly on the unifying character of the message we preach. We Seventh-day Adventists need to recognize our ecumenical responsibility and that its success depends on faithful adherence to, and proclamation of, the biblical truths we hold dear and which alone will bring about this unity. Thus the form of our worship, its liturgical expression, will be effective in the gathering of God's people into one faithful body. Such worship will be effective as an attractive movement toward unity, as a movement of inclusion by which the faithful are identified as those waiting for their Lord in faithfulness and obedience.

In planning the form of our worship, then, we have certain obligations: (1) to the ecumenical character and obligation of the times; (2) to the nature and content of the everlasting gospel; (3) to the tradition of the church to which we belong; and (4) to that which the Spirit would teach us as we are on our way to the marriage feast of the Lamb when His church as bride meets the Bridegroom. The service must have a structure and form that will make worshipers conscious of the three time dimensions of man's existence: past, present, and future.

For Seventh-day Adventist worship this means that the following elements of form are essential:

1. Attention must be drawn to the seventh-day Sabbath on which the congregation gathers for its worship celebration. The Sabbath may be publicized by the preached Word, but it should also be publicized in the other words that are spoken or sung in the order of service itself. The Sabbath reminds us of the past dimension of human existence, of our origin as sons and daughters of God.

2. Attention must be drawn to the heavenly sanctuary and the ministry of Christ there, into which the worshiping congregation has entered by faith. Once again this should be publicized in the elements of the service. It makes us conscious of the present dimension of life, enabling us to see life here in proper relationship to contemporary events in heaven.

3. Attention must be drawn to the second advent of Christ, which is the hope that the congregation takes with it into the world for the following six days. This too should be publicized in the order of service. It provides the future dimension of human existence.

4. The Word of God must be preached. No Adventist worship service should take place without the public proclamation of the eternal gospel, both law and grace. The Seventh-day Adventist Church has a mission of proclamation for which it dare not apologize. It is a message-oriented church, a preaching church, and therefore the communication of the message God has revealed for the end times must be a central feature.

5. The eucharist, or holy communion, must be celebrated on a regular basis. In accordance with the Scriptures the gathered congregation must celebrate the sacramental Word in communion by the eating of bread and the drinking of the unfermented juice of the grape. While the celebration of communion is fixed by Scripture, the details as to how it is to be done are not. For example, it is simply traditional for Adventists to bring the bread and wine to the people in the distribution. An essential part of the service, however, is the washing of feet that is the major focus of John's account of the first communion service. It is in the footwashing that the priesthood of believers is able to function in a dramatic and symbolic way. (See the following chapter.)

6. Whether it takes place in the sanctuary or at a lake or river, baptism is also a major event in Adventist worship. As the symbolic act signifying burial and resurrection with Christ to a new life of faith and obedience, it can never be thought of as an incidental service. It should always take place in the presence of a congregation, or at least a portion of a congregation, as it is not a private affair. It signifies entrance into, and acceptance by, the family of God.

7. Every worship service meets in the name of Jesus Christ, the Creator and Redeemer of the world, for, as He says, "Where two or three come together in my name, there am I with them" (Matt 18:20, NIV).

If the order of service is to do what I have suggested it ought to do, then its form should manifest two structural elements: (1) *constants*—elements that stay the same—, and (2) *variants*—elements that change from week to week. The constants must be limited and must not predominate, but they should always be present for the sake of continuity and familiarity and to form the skeletal structure of the service. In a Seventh-day Adventist order of service the constants could be the introit, the prayer response, and the benedictory response. They are the elements which constitute the liturgical illustration of the Advent message and emphasize the doctrines which identify the Adventist Church and which also provide awareness of the three time dimensions of human life. Though the content of the constants—that is to say, the words themselves—may not be the same from week to week, the intent will remain constant. The introit will focus on the Sabbath, the prayer response on the sanctuary ministry of Christ, and the benedictory response on His second advent. Such repetition is not intrinsically negative. On the contrary, repetition encourages anticipation. For example, in Sibelius's magnificent second symphony the theme is introduced in the first movement and reappears in subtle form throughout until it reaches full expression in the last movement. All the way through the listener anticipates the climax of what he has heard before. Ritual repetition does have power, "the power to revive experience and perhaps even the values that people once may have had, but have lost."[5]

The variants in the worship service are the prelude, invocation, hymns, Scripture reading(s), prayers, sermon, anthems/special music, benediction, and postlude. The offertory response could be included under variants instead of under constants, as one may want to use a different hymn tune from week to week.[6] The variants may or may not be present, usually with the exception of the sermon. For example, there may be an opening prayer in place of the invocation, a closing prayer instead of a benediction. All these elements will vary in relationship to the theme of the day, in contrast to the constants, which would always have a specific liturgical focus as mentioned above.

The introit, prayer response, and benedictory response should not be choral elements alone but congregational elements in the worship service. The function of the choir is to lead the congregation in the singing of hymns and responses rather than to entertain. As a united body the congregation enters into the presence of God in worship. The introit sets the tone of the service; it marks the actual beginning of the worship service and means "entrance." It announces, not the entrance of the clergy onto the platform, but the entrance of the worshiping congregation into the presence of God. Worship leaders should be in their places on the platform when the introit is sung.

The prayer response is the liturgical illustration and reminder that the congregation has entered the heavenly sanctuary by faith. Christ their High Priest hears their prayers and intercedes before the Father on their behalf. The benedictory response is the liturgical illustration and reminder that the congregation, which has been in God's presence, heard His Word, and received grace and power to live its faith in the world, now has the mission to evangelize the world and so participate in the preparations to meet Christ when He comes in glory.

[5]Frank C. Senn, *Christian Worship and Its Cultural Setting* (Philadelphia: Fortress Press, 1983), p. 3.

[6]See Appendix A.

The introit, prayer response, and benedictory response are musical elements in the worship service and are sung by choir and congregation, or congregation alone. In addition to the singing of hymns and anthems they provide additional opportunity for the ministry of music to function.

The Role of Music in Worship

Worship can only be done by believers. It is not so much an appeal as a response. The language spoken in worship is addressed primarily to God, even though in Scripture reading and sermon He speaks to His people. But words alone are not enough. A full worship service on a Sabbath morning without music, without singing, is dull and dead. Throughout the biblical account worship includes the sounds of musical instruments, and the best instrument of all for praise is the human voice. Music is, therefore, an integral part of Christian worship. John the revelator describes this music and singing as the "new song" (Rev 5:9–13). Music dramatizes the transcendence of God and draws the worshiper into the heavenly sanctuary. It serves to pull forth from deep within the worshiper that sense of awe and mystery most appropriate to Christian worship. It dramatizes the mystery of the church as a fellowship, as the congregation lifts united voices in song.[7] Like nothing else in the worship service, music stimulates participation. For this reason, music in a liturgical context should not be primarily a performance by specialists. Music exists to help the congregation exercise its priestly ministry in worship. The congregation sings its faith to itself and in the process contributes to the building of faith. There is no exhilaration to match that of a believing congregation singing its faith in, and praise to, God.

Music in worship provides a degree of intensity that words alone cannot evoke. It helps the spoken word achieve an even greater power of expression. It helps the worshiper acknowledge and express a deeper level of reality, and makes possible a response of the total self to the presence and Word of God. Furthermore, music helps the believer to express the inexpressible. It does not exist for itself alone. It is not autonomous. It must always be subordinated to the Word and glory of God. It is not for entertaining the people, but to help them glorify God, and is for the fostering of spirituality, not simply aesthetics. It is to assist the human voice, as an "expression of a conscious personality," to celebrate the presence of God.[8] It makes possible the singing of faith

[7]For a discussion of the role of sound in worship see Robert E. Webber, *Worship Old and New* (Grand Rapids, Mich.: Zondervan, 1982), pp. 175–183.

[8]Paquier, *Dynamics of Worship*, p. 151.

to the God who has given faith. But there is also a place for *jubilus*—praise without words—when the organ and/or instruments continue the praise that has been evoked by the Word, as voices are stilled by the majesty of God. This phenomenon is most appropriate at the close of the service as tacit permission is given by the congregation for the instrument(s) to serve as the extension of the human voice.

Nevertheless, all church music is secondary to congregational singing. One of the greatest examples of hymn singing in the Bible is in chapters 4–5 of Revelation, where in the form of a *sanctus* and *doxologies*, praise is given to the God who created the world and the Son of God who redeemed the world. From the verbal chorus of chapter 4 the expression progresses to the climactic singing of chapter 5, when the response is to the gospel of salvation and redemption. Here is a dramatic description of worship in heaven, the kind of worship in which God's people will participate following the return of the Lord. It is reminiscent of the great singing done by the people of God on the day the wall of Jerusalem was dedicated in Nehemiah's time. On that occasion two massed choirs participated in the service. They took their places in the house of God, together with officials and the priests with their trumpets, and sang under the direction of one Jezrahiah. "And on that day they offered great sacrifices, rejoicing because God has given them great joy. The women and children also rejoiced. The sound of rejoicing in Jerusalem could be heard far away" (Neh 14:43, NIV). There should be much praise and much rejoicing in Seventh-day Adventist worship. The song of instruments and the song of human voices should join together in praise of Him who has redeemed us and saved us for His kingdom and will soon come to take us to be with Him!

The psalter certainly presents biblical evidence that music and singing are integral to the experience of worship. In fact music itself can be a form of worship. That is to say, it can be directed toward God rather than to the people. If music can be for God, then it behooves the church not to offer Him mediocrity and/or pure sentimentalism. The fact is that the level of music in the church can rise no higher than our understanding of its role and its importance. Such understanding is essential for pastors as well as musicians. Musicians should be encouraged to give the best of their vocation as they lead the church to greater appreciation for good music in worship. But church musicians and pastors need to be alert to the fact that "music in the service of the Church is not at its best when it is trying to be master; but neither is it at its best when it is made a slave."[9] Those who are responsible for the

[9]Segler, *Christian Worship: Its Theology and Practice*, p. 100.

music ministry in the church must not function dictatorially, but in harmony with the feelings and taste of the congregation. At the same time the congregation should encourage organists and choir directors, ministers of music, to give of their best to the musical expression of worship. There may very well be a need for growth in sanctification when it comes to musical taste and usage both in family and corporate worship. If we can work toward and achieve a balance regarding music in the liturgical life of the church, we will be making great progress in learning to appreciate the gifts God has given to His church, and in learning how best to use those gifts harmoniously in fulfilling the mutual ministry we have been given.

Music is not an end in itself, but exists for the people of the church to express their faith in God and to glorify Him in worship. The words of James F. White say it best: "Since I am a liturgist, I am prone to feel that the musician has been the victim of his own musical excellence. Should he want less than the very best he would not be worth his pay, meager as that usually is. But what is best for offering our worship, music of the highest aesthetic quality or music of a singable and relevant variety? Too long we have operated on a notion that what was best could be distinguished by careful rules. We could say Bach was good and Sullivan was not because of certain standards. But we did not always bother to say good for what or for whom. This led to an aesthetic snobbery that meant we thought we knew what was good for everyone. We adopted a like-it-or-leave-it attitude which is no better in worship than it is in patriotism. How important then are aesthetic standards? They are extremely important in distinguishing between the various possibilities on the same level of musical accomplishment and difficulty. But even more important is the concern that music be for the people. In worship, music ought to be judged in terms of people, not people in terms of music."[10]

Because hymns and the act of corporate singing have a unifying effect, which we certainly want to appreciate and foster, worship leaders must not fail to give attention to the relationship between theology and music in worship. Hymn singing not only serves as the corporate affirmation of faith, it also serves to teach the doctrines of the church. While hymn singing can meet human needs on the deepest level of human experience, at the same time it can affirm the objective truth upon which faith and religious experience rest. Thus the kinds of hymns we choose for our worship service must take into account doctrinal content as well as singability and musical excellence.

[10]James E. White, *New Forms of Worship* (Nashville: Abingdon, 1971), pp. 128–129.

The Adventist Church is taking steps in the right direction. The establishment of the Oliver Beltz Professorship of Sacred Music in the Theological Seminary at Andrews University is a major development, and the teaching of hymnology in a formal and scholarly way is beginning to find its rightful place in the seminary curriculum. This, in a significant way, should contribute to a gradual reformation of musical tastes in the church. The proposal to the General Conference to establish an Office of Worship and Church Music at an administrative level is another significant step. Perhaps in due time serious consideration might be given to the development of curricula leading to an M.Div. major in church music as a prerequisite to the eventual ordination of ministers of music in our church.

These developments all give evidence of an emerging reexamination of worship in the Seventh-day Adventist Church, together with a renewed appreciation of the role of music and musicians in the life of the church. This reexamination and renewal can bring deeper significance and greater beauty to Adventist worship services. The order of service can be likened to a musical score. As the score helps the musician know what notes to play, and when, so the order of service helps the people of God know how to sing the new song.

Discussion Questions

1. What planning should be done to help educate congregations as to the meaning of SDA liturgical symbols in worship?
2. How can a congregation become involved in reducing liturgical ambiguity?
3. Which parts of the order of service should be focused on the Deity, and which focused on the people?
4. When it comes to the choice and use of music in worship, which shall prevail: aesthetics or individual taste and opinion?

Worship and Footwashing / 9

The Seventh-day Adventist Church shares the great Christian tradition of worship as the basic expression of faith and religious experience. On this side of the resurrection it is in worship that doctrine becomes clothed, becomes identifiable. We understand what a church believes by what it does or does not do in its worship services. Worship provides the opportunity for God's people to publicly express their faith, and also to declare their identity. The nature of our worship reveals who we are.

A significant part of our worship life is holy communion, discussed in chapter 7. A very important part of the communion service for Seventh-day Adventists is footwashing, which we take very seriously and practice regularly. For that reason we ought to have some idea of the relationship between what we believe about footwashing and what we do when we practice it. This discussion is included here as an illustration of what has been said in previous chapters concerning the liturgical dramatization of what we believe. Footwashing, as commonly practiced, does not always do this.

Theological Meaning

My first encounters with footwashing were disappointing, to say the least. Even today, after thirteen years as an Adventist minister, participation in footwashing often leaves me disappointed. This is not because the service has no intrinsic meaning. On the contrary, it has rich biblical significance. But that significance does not always find adequate liturgical expression. In other words, what is said and done during the footwashing service very often does not express and illustrate what we believe about it.

For example, the conversations that occur between the men with whom I am participating often have nothing at all to do with what we are doing. The talk is about baseball, the weather, politics both national and ecclesiastical, church business, secular business, work, etc.—anything except what we are actually doing in washing feet. The whole thing seems to be nothing more than ritual, with little or no attention paid to what is going on. It seems, often, to be something that is suffered in a detached sort of way in preparation for holy communion. To one who has been trained to appreciate the relationship between doctrine and liturgical action, footwashing appears to be treated as a meaningless ritual.

Like the members of congregations, I find myself resisting participation at times. Frequently, while pastoring, I would receive phone calls from members of other Adventist churches inquiring if my church was having a communion service the next Sabbath. If I replied in the negative the caller was pleased to announce that he/she would visit my church that day. It was increasingly obvious that communion Sabbath was a good time to go visiting. I began to wonder if some of those people were feeling the way I was about footwashing.

When I do participate I find myself wondering why we men do it at all. Our conduct and conversation often indicate that the footwashing service is quite meaningless. When I became the pastor of an Adventist Church I realized my pastoral responsibility to teach my congregation the meaning of the liturgical action of footwashing. I could not blame the participants for their indifference, and I resisted the temptation to preach a rip-snorting, flock-flogging sermon about it. What was lacking was not the need for footwashing, or the desire to participate, but understanding of its significance and the translation of significance into practice. For that I was responsible as pastor and worship leader.

As a responsible Adventist pastor, then, I began to explore for meaning, looking into both the Bible and the writings of Ellen G. White. It was during a study of Mrs. White's theology of footwashing, particularly in chapter 71 of *Desire of Ages*, that I became intrigued by the account in the Gospel of John, chapter 13. John is the only Gospel writer who gives us details of the footwashing episode as a part of the Last Supper and as part of the institution of holy communion. Instead of lessening communion's impact, as some believe, the description of footwashing serves instead to increase it. Evidently the Lord thought this episode so important that the Holy Spirit made certain it was included in the inspired record.

In chapter 13 John speaks of the washing of the feet of the disciples and of the fact that this washing had to do with their having a "part" with the Lord (verse 8). This implies a participation in what He came to do, a participation in ministry. He gave His disciples an example of service and chose them (verse 18) for that service. This is emphasized again in verse 20 when He said, as part of His explanation of His actions in washing their feet, "Truly, truly, I say to you, he who receives any one whom I send receives me; and he who receives me receives Him who sent me." It is apparent that a "sending" is involved in the washing. In what sense?

The key to understanding this sending may be found in the account of the ordaining of Aaron and his sons to the priesthood. In Ex 29:1 we read: "Now this is what you shall do to consecrate them, that they may serve me as priests." Then the Lord continues with His instructions as to the manner in which Aaron and his sons are to be set apart. In verse 4 God tells Moses, "You shall bring Aaron and his sons to the door of the tent of meeting, and wash them with water." Lev 8:6 indicates that it was done. They were also to be anointed: "And you shall anoint Aaron and his sons, and consecrate them, that they may serve me as priests" (Ex 30:30; see also Ex 28:41; 40:13–15). Lev 8:10–12 and Num 3:3 record the anointing as having been done. So there was a washing and an anointing as part of the ordaining or setting apart of Aaron and his sons as priests of the Lord.

When it came to the liturgy of the tabernacle, God gave special instructions concerning the washing required as preparation for the sanctuary services: "The Lord said to Moses, 'You shall take a laver of bronze, with the base of bronze, for washing. And you shall put it between the tent of meeting and the altar, and you shall put water in it, with which Aaron and his sons shall wash their hands and feet. When they go into the tent of meeting or when they come near to the altar to minister, to burn an offering by fire to the Lord, they shall wash with water lest they die. They shall wash their hands and feet lest they die' " (Ex 30:17–21). In Lev 16:4, 24, and 28, God, in giving the liturgy of the Day of Atonement, orders that Aaron "shall bathe his body in water." Thus, by washing, Aaron and his sons were set apart and ordained and prepared for the priesthood. Washing also became a part of the ministrations of the priesthood in the sanctuary.

The letter to the Hebrews refers to the Lord Jesus Christ as High Priest. In John 12:1–3 we are told He was anointed, and John 1, Luke 3, Mark 1, and Matthew 3 testify that He was washed in the Jordan by the Baptist. Washed and anointed, Jesus was ready for His priestly ministry.

In washing the disciples' feet the Lord, as High Priest, was setting them apart, ordaining them, for ministry. That ministry was to be priests to all people and to serve as He served. His act was both example and commission. He was setting them apart as well as illustrating the nature of their ministry. When He said, "If I do not wash you, you have no part in me," He meant much more than fellowship with Him by faith. He meant also participation in the proclamation of His kingdom by means of word and deed. They were set apart to have a part in that ministry in the same way that Aaron and his sons were set apart. However, it would not be until Pentecost that they would fully realize what had taken place and would receive the divine power, the anointing, to perform their ministries as He had prophesied when He told them in the eucharistic discourse, "Truly, truly, I say to you, he who believes in me will also do the works that I do; and greater works than these will he do, because I go to the Father. Whatever you ask in my name, I will do it, that the Father may be glorified in the Son; if you ask anything in my name, I will do it" (John 14:12–13).

Thus, as we participate in footwashing we do so not only in response to the Lord's example, but also in acknowledgment of the priestly ministry received from Him for one another and for the world. The footwashing service is a fitting preparation for participation in the sacrament of the Lord's body and blood, from which we also receive divine grace to perform our ministries.

It was immediately after the commissioning of the disciples by washing their feet that the Lord launched into His eucharistic discourse, which had a definite eschatological message. He reminded His disciples that He would be leaving them, that He would not leave them comfortless, that He would be going to prepare a place for them, and that He would come again to take them to Himself. This eschatological emphasis of the eucharist is experienced when the believer, in loving obedience and by means of God's grace, fulfills Christ's commission to "make disciples of all nations . . . until the close of the age" (Matt 28:19–20).

The footwashing, understood in the sense of preparation for fellowship and ministry, is not an addendum to the Lord's Supper: It is not another separate ordinance. It is, rather, an integral part of the communion service. In the footwashing our Lord as anointed High Priest is setting us apart for the priesthood of all believers which He intends us to fulfill daily until He comes again. We are to do for one another what He has done for mankind: give of ourselves in loving service and ministry. To prepare to meet Him is not to sit and wait, but to wait in active service as He indicates in the entire 25th chapter of the Gospel of Matthew.

Jesus, on the eve of His departure, wanted to leave His disciples some final instruction and inspiration. He had been teaching them by word of mouth. Now He chose a most dramatic illustration—washing their feet—by which to impress upon them His great concern: that they care for each other and minister to each other after His departure. This demonstration taught them the manner in which the church, His body, would function. Only as its members dedicated themselves to ministry could the church be made strong to keep the faith and spread the Gospel.

"He had a full consciousness of His divinity," Ellen White says of the Lord, "but He had laid aside His royal crown and kingly robes, and had taken the form of a servant. One of the last acts of His life on earth was to gird Himself as a servant and perform a servant's part."[1] The response of Judas to this role of Christ as servant provides another insight into the meaning of the footwashing service. As Jesus washed Judas' feet, Judas had the impulse to confess his sin then and there, but he would not humble himself and hardened his heart against repentance. Evidently repentance and confession are a part of being washed! Christ served Judas, the betrayer, first. The greatest sinner can be washed clean and made usable by the Saviour. When Peter refused to let Jesus wash his feet he was refusing his Lord and the higher cleansing as well as the Lord's ministry.

Liturgical Meaning

Speaking of the people of Israel at the time of their deliverance from Egypt and the institution of the Passover meal (the forerunner of Christian communion), Ellen White says: "The manner in which they celebrated this ordinance harmonized with their condition."[2] How were they to celebrate it? "Now you shall eat it in this manner: with your loins girded, your sandals on your feet, and your staff in your hand; and you shall eat it in haste—it is the Lord's passover" (Ex 12:11). The liturgical symbolism is that of a sinful people in need of redemption, and who are to be ready at any time to fulfill the divine will. So the manner of observance is linked with belief, doctrine, theology, and condition. The condition of the disciples at the time of the first footwashing was one of contention and competition. James and John had requested to sit at the Lord's right hand in His kingdom and this stirred the indignation of the others. Alienation was a very real threat. Hearts were full of resentment and jealousy. With such attitudes it was impossible for any of them to seriously consider assuming the role of a servant. They all "manifested a stoical unconcern."[3]

[1]White, *Desire of Ages*, p. 645.
[2]Ibid., p. 653.
[3]Ibid., p. 644.

Jesus demonstrated the meaning of the gospel in interpersonal relationships between believers. He "laid aside his garments" (see Phil 2:4–8), "girded himself with a towel," and "poured water into a basin." He did it all! Then He "began to wash the disciples' feet and to wipe them with the towel with which he was girded." The disciples had already been "washed in the great fountain opened for sin and uncleanness."[4] But now Jesus would wash from their hearts the alienation, jealousy, and pride that had a negative and destructive effect on their relationships with each other as well as a negative effect on their relationship with Jesus. Until this happened they were not ready for corporate communion with Christ.

Because of Christ's actions, the disciples were led to think differently and feel differently about each other. So it is with Christians today. "Whenever this ordinance is rightly celebrated, the children of God are brought into a holy relationship to help and bless each other."[5] But there is a condition to this holy relationship: the ordinance must be "rightly celebrated." There must be a right celebration as opposed to a wrong celebration if help and blessing are to be experienced. This "right celebration" has to do with the form footwashing takes as well as with what the church believes about footwashing. Liturgical ambiguity is a problem with many of our Sabbath morning services because the action of the congregation in worship is often not in harmony with the words that are spoken. The opposite is the case when it comes to our footwashing services. The liturgical action is assured by the very nature of the service. We cannot participate in footwashing without going through the repetitive ritual actions of girding, pouring, and washing. What is missing is the right word. If either the right word or the right action is missing, the consequence is ambiguity. We are left with *only* ritual.

In the footwashing service "the holy watcher from heaven is present at this season to make it one of soul searching, of conviction of sin, and of the blessed assurance of sins forgiven."[6] The outcome, or existential result, of footwashing should be the *assurance of sins forgiven.* How does that happen? Does it happen simply because we have engaged in the ritual, the liturgical action? Does the washing away of sin inhere in the water used? In the willingness to submit? In the drying of the feet? Do these acts alone assure the convicted, repentant soul that his sins are truly forgiven?

[4]White, *Desire of Ages*, p. 646.
[5]Ibid., p. 651.
[6]Ibid., p. 650.

In Roman Catholic sacramental theology it is believed that forgiveness comes simply by participating in the ritual of communion. The sacrament works *ex opera operato*, in and by itself. As long as sacraments are offered by a properly ordained priest they are effective. In contrast to that concept of the priestly role is the Protestant concept of the priesthood of all believers, the idea that every Christian is called to serve as a priest to his fellow believers and to his fellow men. This priesthood does not only have reference to an individual coming to the Lord without an intermediary. It has reference to ministry to and for each other within the church. We can offer nothing to God on another's behalf, in contrast to the Roman Catholic concept of priestly power, but we can offer to each other what God has given to His people, the true treasure of the church: the gospel and all its promises of divine mercy and grace. The true apostolic succession is not the passing on of exclusive priestly power from one hierarchical figure to another. It is the passing of the gospel from one believer to another in the form of "sound words" (2 Tim 1:13, 14; 2:1–2). This priesthood every Christian believer has received by virtue of the new birth, baptism, and the anointing of the Holy Spirit.

Therefore, no assurance of forgiveness is possible unless the Word of the gospel is ministered, for faith comes from hearing this Word (Rom 10:17). The gospel must be spoken and heard. Unless that happens, ritual is ambiguous and has no meaning. Footwashing is a gracious opportunity provided for the members of the body of Christ to exercise the priesthood of all believers and minister the Word of God personally to one another.

In this regard Dietrich Bonhoeffer makes the following remarks: "Where Christians live together the time must inevitably come when in some crisis one person will have to declare God's Word and will to another. It is inconceivable that the things that are of utmost importance to each individual should not be spoken by one to another," and, "He has put His Word in our mouth. He wants it to be spoken through us. If we hinder His Word, the blood of the sinning brother will be upon us. If we carry out His Word, God will save our brother through us."[7] Not to speak His Word, not to share His Word, is to hinder it. Commenting on Bonhoeffer's remarks, Clyde Fant says: "We must also learn the discipline of listening to God's Word from others."[8] Here we are confronted with the power of the spoken Word.

[7]Dietrich Bonhoeffer, *Life Together*, trans. John W. Doberstein (New York: Harper & Bros., 1954), pp. 105, 108.

[8]Clyde E. Fant, *Bonhoeffer: Worldly Preaching* (Nashville: Thomas Nelson Inc., 1975), p. 29.

In order for me to approach the Lord's Supper knowing that my sins are forgiven, I must hear the word of forgiveness. This might well take place during the footwashing in the following conversational manner. Kneeling at the feet of the one whom I will wash, I might ask, "What are your spiritual needs today?" He might answer, "I have been struggling with a sin that has been bothering me for some time." My response: "Would you like me to pray the Lord to grant you victory over that sin?" Upon his affirmative answer we would bow our heads together as I prayed for him; then I might either read or quote 1 John 1:9, which would be the word of forgiveness and assurance he needs from God: "If we confess our sins, he is faithful and just and will forgive us our sins and purify us from all unrighteousness" (NIV). Regarding confession Ellen White wrote: "To those to whom it is proper, who will take no advantage of your wrong, confess according to the word of God, and let them pray for you, and God will accept your work and will heal you."[9] This is why it is best to share footwashing with someone we know rather than with a total stranger. It is preferable to find our own partner rather than have one selected for us by a deacon or deaconess. The best way is to make the arrangement with the one who will be our partner well in advance of the communion service.

The conversation may not go exactly as the one described above. Other equally significant and troubling matters may be included. Or the footwashing service could be a time of praising and rejoicing together. Adventists are trained to be biblically literate people and ought to be able to find or quote from memory pertinent Bible passages that meet the existing need. On occasions when such passages may not readily come to mind, surely one's general Bible knowledge can be brought into play in the ministry of assurance.

It could be objected that the spoken word is not necessary in connection with footwashing in order to be assured of forgiveness, that if one's heart asks God for cleansing at that time it is sufficient, for the act of footwashing is but symbolic. But the footwashing in connection with the Lord's Supper is more than a symbol. It did not merely point to a higher cleansing, but, as Ellen White says, the higher cleansing is "included in the lower."[10] Those who participate "receive Christ's words."[11] It is inconceivable that assurance of forgiveness could be experienced in a footwashing context in which all kinds of words

[9]White, *Testimonies for the Church*, Vol. 2, p. 296.
[10]White, *Desire of Ages*, p. 646.
[11]Ibid.

unrelated to the event itself are spoken. Is it not more important that one hears the Word of God rather than words related to other concerns? Without such a word transaction the experience would be totally subjective and individualistic and not a part of the corporate life of the body of Christ.

Humility becomes part of this service when I allow my brother to act as Christ's servant to me, when I confess, repent, admit my need for cleansing, and then eagerly hear the good news of forgiveness. The one who does the washing must submit to being used as a servant, taking Christ's place, serving as a channel of grace and blessing and as a minister of the Word. The one who is washed must receive the ministry. But it is the Word of God alone that gives life and joy and peace.

The language of John 13:20 is similar to that of Matthew 25:41ff. To permit, in an attitude of confession and repentance and faith, a fellow believer to wash your feet is to receive Christ. He said it. We must take Him at His word.

I don't know *how* it happens—when we try to figure that out we end up caught in theological cobwebs—but I know *that* it happens when the Word is ministered because the Word itself says so. The Word of God does something to me as well as tells me something. That is the nature of all language. When the Lord speaks through His Word He speaks creatively and what He says actually happens. It is in the ability to speak to one another that humans reflect part of the image of God. What more powerful word is there to speak than the Word of God?

Ellen White says footwashing is a "memorial of His humiliation."[12] It is not a memorial of our humiliation. To participate in it is to renounce our self-centeredness and insensitivity, to renounce our false humility which so often is disguised pride, to renounce our competitiveness and struggle for greatness, and to participate in His ministry of loving and sacrificial service. The greatest thing Christians can do for each other is to share the promises of the gospel in sympathetic understanding. In the words of Paul Tournier, "Our vocation is to reply to human suffering."[13] Our footwashing liturgy ought to make that priestly ministry possible.

Verses 14, 15, and 17 of John 13 indicate that footwashing was not to be an activity reserved only for the twelve apostles. It was intended to become a part of the Christian community's celebration of the Lord's Supper. It was to be included in the liturgical action of the

[12]White, *Desire of Ages*, p. 650.

[13]Paul Tournier, *Guilt and Grace* (New York: Harper and Row, 1962), p. 59.

worshiping church that is waiting for the return of its Lord and engaged in the process of building itself up in love and service.

"Blessed are those servants whom the Master finds awake when He comes; truly, I say to you, he will gird himself and have them sit at table, and he will come and serve them" (Luke 12:37). We talk about serving Christ—but can you imagine what is in store for us when He returns and once again serves us? The Word of God promises it! That service is not our reward for being good people. It is the extension of the ministry of the One who gave Himself as a ransom for many and who loves us "to the end" (John 13:1). By His grace He is preparing a people for that blessed experience as we participate in the footwashing service that allows us to serve and be served.

Discussion Questions

1. What relationship does footwashing have to the priesthood of believers?
2. How can we best practice footwashing in ways that reflect what we believe about it?
3. Is there any biblical, theological, social, psychological rationale for husbands and wives participating in the footwashing service together?
4. How can we guard against footwashing becoming just another ritual?

Worship and Child Dedications / 10

As Seventh-day Adventists we do not baptize infants; we dedicate them instead. Churches which practice infant baptism believe that God acts in baptism and claims the child as His own apart from the child's own faith, or they believe that baptism generates faith. Seventh-day Adventists, together with many other Christian people, believe that parents must willingly offer their children as gifts to the care of God. It is the faith of the parents as members of the body of Christ that is operative. Both views are attempts to acknowledge liturgically that God's love and grace extend to His care for the smallest of His creatures.

In any discussion of the liturgical symbolism of a child dedication service we need to take into account what we believe about the church, the pastoral role, the role of the father as household priest, the role of the mother, and the priesthood of all believers. Once again what we believe should be illustrated in our liturgical practice.

The Role of Minister and Parents

The New Testament makes no hard-and-fast distinctions between church members and clergymen. The term "laity" is used in reference to every person who has taken his stand for Christ and the gospel, including ministers. Ministers are a part of the laity, not separate from it. They are a part of the people of God. Gottfried Oosterwal writes: "By virtue of their baptism, in principle, all members participate alike in the apostolic succession (authority, in the priesthood), in the ministry, in the worship, in the mission, and in the charismata (gifts) of the church."[1]

[1]Gottfried Oosterwal, *Mission Possible* (Nashville: Southern Publishing Association, 1967), p. 110.

Any differences that exist between members of the body of Christ are seen in terms of services rendered and not in terms of hierarchical status.

In Eph 4:12 it is clear that God has called the laity "for the work of ministry." The role of apostles, prophets, evangelists, pastors, and teachers is to assist each other in equipping the members for that work. In other words, these services are intended to make possible the ministry of the laity. That is the function the pastor performs in child dedications. He makes it possible for the priesthood of all believers, the ministry of the laity, to be exercised. He also organizes the service in such a way that this ministry of the laity is illustrated liturgically.

Seventh-day Adventist ministers do not function in child dedications in the same way a Catholic priest would function in an infant baptism. In Catholicism the priest baptizes the baby. In Adventism the minister does not dedicate the baby or child. He does not have that kind of power and authority, any more than the Christian church has the power and authority to sanctify Sunday as its holy day. God alone sanctifies. God alone sets apart for His use. That is actually what happens in child dedications. The child is set apart for the Lord's care and service.

While the minister may be the representative of the body of Christ, let him exercise that task as an enabler rather than by usurping to himself a function of ministry that belongs to the people. In the case of child dedications, that function belongs to the father, who, as head of the family, is their priest. It is really the parents who dedicate their children and not ministers. I have no right, as a minister, to dedicate someone else's children. Those children have not been given to me for stewardship of their upbringing and nurture. They have been given by the Lord to their natural parents through the miracle of conception and birth. The parents are therefore stewards of that life. They, and they alone, can exercise that stewardship by offering their child to the care and service of the Lord and the gospel.

That dedication ought to take place in the presence of the whole congregation. The congregation needs to have its responsibility for the child's nurture in the faith dramatized and illustrated. In dedication the child is acknowledged to be a part of the family of God, the church. As an object of God's love and care, the child is to be loved and cared for by the whole family of God.

In child dedication services we have another opportunity to proclaim and illustrate what we believe theologically by our liturgical action.

Liturgical Illustration

First of all, the service of dedication should be made the central feature in the worship hour. It should not be an addendum, something tacked on and given the impression of an afterthought or intrusion. The hymns, the Scripture readings, the prayers, the sermon, the anthem or special music, as variants, ought to reflect the significance and harmonize with the theme of the occasion. Child dedication is a significant event in the life of any congregation. It must be utilized by the minister to once again proclaim and illustrate the church's faith.

Second, the minister's role is that of enabling the ministry of the laity and the priesthood of all believers to function. The minister must carefully instruct the congregation as to the symbolic meaning of the liturgical action in which they will participate. In that way they are included and learn to appreciate the relationship between theology and liturgy. In the liturgical structure of the dedication service it becomes possible for lay ministry to become operative. In harmony with the belief that the minister's role is not to dedicate but to facilitate, the parents are called forward at the appropriate moment in the worship service. The father is instructed to carry the child in his arms. He then places the child in the minister's arms, liturgically symbolizing the act of the parents in offering their child to the Lord in thanksgiving. The father then, as priest of the family, rightfully offers the dedicatory prayer. He should take the hand of his wife, the child's mother, when he does this, thus symbolizing family solidarity and responsibility.

Two references to the act of child dedication are found in the writings of Ellen G. White. They are both the same. "Let ministers of the Gospel take the little children in their arms and bless them in the name of Jesus."[2] This injunction is fulfilled in the liturgical action described above. There is, however, ample room for creativity and innovation within that injunction. The child in the pastor's arms is symbolic of its having been received by the heavenly Father and blessed thereby. The minister then returns the child into the mother's arms in liturgical fulfillment of the injunction: "Let mothers now lead their children to Christ."[3] This further symbolizes the fact that God is now returning the child to its parents so they can exercise their parental stewardship and care in His stead.

[2]Ellen G. White, *The Adventist Home* (Nashville: Southern Publishing Association, 1952), p. 174; *Evangelism* (Washington: Review and Herald Publishing Association, 1946), p. 349.

[3]White, *Adventist Home*, p. 274.

At that point in the service the congregation should be admonished as to its corporate responsibility for the nurturing of that child in the faith. Appropriate Scripture passages may be cited and references to the church's responsibility for providing schools for its youth may be made. Members are exhorted to be the kind of model Christians the child needs as examples of Christian living and witness.

The sermon presents the minister with the opportunity to further elaborate on the theme of the day, which should be some aspect of family life.

Discussion Questions

1. Can you think of other ways, than those mentioned above, by which what we believe theologically about child dedication can be illustrated liturgically?

Adventist Worship and the Ministry of the Word in Mission

Part Four

Worship and Preaching / 11

All through the history of Christianity the pendulum has swung back and forth when it comes to the place of preaching in worship. It is not so strange that this has been so. Opposition and uncertainty regarding Christ have been reflected in uncertainty and opposition regarding preaching. The incarnation of God in Christ was a new development in faith and revelation. With the ascension of the Lord and the coming of the Holy Spirit to continue the Lord's ministry on earth, a new form of communication of the Word of God came into being. On Pentecost the gospel was first publicly proclaimed. This proclamation was called preaching. Religious dialogue took place between the disciples who believed and people who were outside the faith. In preaching the divine Word would be communicated by means of the human word. *The Word* would be transmitted through the words of men.

The Centrality of Preaching

The revised *Manual for Church Officers*, reflecting the philosophy of ministry of the document entitled "Evangelism and Finishing God's Work" voted by the Annual Council in 1976, indicates that the Seventh-day Adventist pastor has four major responsibilities for which he receives salary and is responsible: preaching, shepherding, training, and evangelizing.[1] It is obvious that these four are interrelated functions of ministry, and that all are directly related to church growth. But it is highly significant that preaching stands at the top of the list, thus indicating the belief of the church that preaching is the primary

[1]*Manual for Church Officers* (Washington: Ministerial Association, General Conference of Seventh-day Adventists, 1978), pp. 47–51.

responsibility of the SDA minister, and that preaching has a direct bearing on the other three. It has been my personal conviction for many years that spiritual life, church growth in terms of building the faith life of members and winning new members to the faith, is directly related to the kind of preaching heard Sabbath to Sabbath from our pulpits. There is truth to the adage that as preaching goes, so goes the church. It is even more true to say that as preachers go, so goes the church.

When one thinks about worship one of the first thoughts is about the sermon, about the activity of the called servant in serving as the bridge between the ancient Word and the contemporary context of human life. But preaching has not always been held in high favor. During the liturgical revival of the 1950s and 1960s opinions concerning preaching hit a new low. In fact there were those who believed it should be abandoned altogether, classifying it as an outmoded and no longer relevant or useful method of reaching the hearts of people. All kinds of comunication innovations appeared on the worship scene to take the place of what has historically been called the sermon, religious drama and multi-media presentations being the most common. The dialogue sermon also came into vogue in which two speakers conversed in the presence of a congregation.

I recall many discussions with fellow seminary students in those days when it was argued strenuously that sermons ought not be more than ten to fifteen minutes in length, if that long. Sermonizing should be minimized and the sacraments maximized, it was thought. This view was reflected in the meager preaching diet we seminarians received from the pulpit of the seminary chapel. Most Protestant churches had forgotten what Martin Luther and the other sixteenth-century reformers had fought so hard to achieve: the restoration of preaching to a central position in the belief that no Christian congregation should gather for worship without the proclamation of the Word of God. The Seventh-day Adventist Church, however, is still committed to the centrality of preaching in the worship of God's people (2 Tim 4:2–5).

Yet there is always the danger that the pendulum will be allowed to swing too far in the other direction and that we will lose sight of the significance of the other elements of worship for the sake of biblical exposition. If the sermon is to be what it is meant to be, it can never be thought of as an isolated event in the church's worship. It will achieve its greatest significance only as a part of a worship service rich in music and the liturgical symbols of congregational action.

Preaching (and listening to preaching) is never an isolated event. It takes place in the context of life as well as in the context of a worship service. It is part of the celebration of the Word of God and the celebration of human life. We are fortunate, as Adventists, to have retained our belief in the centrality of preaching, because the 1970s witnessed a resurgence of interest in effective pulpit communication. Even though this renewed interest in preaching can largely be attributed to the humanistic influence in contemporary theology, in which Christianity is seen primarily as the celebration of life, we can be grateful for what has been happening.

During ten years as a Lutheran minister I decried the swing away from preaching in the direction of sacramentalism. For many the way in which the minister held his hands during the distribution of communion was more important and significant than his expository ability. For me, during those years, preaching was always the most important ministerial function. Though set in an elaborate and old liturgical tradition, I still felt preaching to be the high point of the worship service, in spite of the pressure exerted by many of my ministerial colleagues who insisted that communion was the high point. It was not difficult for me, therefore, to make the transition to the Adventist ministry, where the pulpit is the focal center of the sanctuary and where the congregation eagerly awaits the proclamation of the Word of God. During the past thirteen years as an Adventist minister I have been able to indulge to the fullest extent what I have long believed was the Protestant tradition concerning preaching. I was no longer criticized by my contemporaries for the personal goal of excellence in preaching ability. It was now welcomed, encouraged, and appreciated. I felt more free to do what I believed I was called and trained and ordained to do: preach the Word.

However, I am now bothered by references to worship as the "preaching service." I still retain deep appreciation for congregational prayer, the corporate singing of hymns, the reading of the Scriptures, and the best possible Christian music, all organized and planned in such a way that the sermon is elevated to a position it would not have otherwise. Preaching is to be central, yes, but it is not the only significant activity taking place in worship. It is to be the central feature in a service rich in Adventist liturgical action that reflects what we are as a people. We have rich doctrinal traditions which need to be illustrated in worship. To do so will enhance and elevate the preaching of the Word in which those doctrines are revealed. When the worship service is enriched liturgically the sermon does not disappear. The preaching of the Word is enhanced and elevated when it takes place within an order of service that prepares the congregation for that moment. Preaching is degraded when it is simply one part of a hodge-podge of unrelated activity. Effective preaching, as part of the worship service, should have the following characteristics which contribute to a meaningful worship experience for the listener.

Preaching as Timely and Timeless

The preacher's task is awesome. In the context of a worship service, it is his responsibility to serve as the verbal connection between the ancient and revealed Word of God and the lives of the worshipers, who live in a far different age than that of the Bible writers. His preaching, therefore, needs to be both timeless and timely.

The man of God must master the Scriptures as God's revealed source of truth concerning Himself, the world, mankind, life in general, history, and the plan of salvation and its final outcome. He has been charged with the communication of the timeless truths of God. There is information in the Scriptures which God desires to be clearly and concisely communicated to the waiting congregation. So the preacher must be prepared to speak as a prophet from time to time, to say, "Thus says the Lord." This requires deep and thorough study of the Scriptures. Such study takes time. The old rule of thumb was that for every minute in the pulpit there should be one hour of study and preparation. Thus a thirty-minute sermon would have thirty hours of study behind it. It may not be practical to spend that much time each week in sermon preparation, but a faithful and dedicated pastor should be able to spend at least fifteen hours a week getting ready for the primary task of preaching to his flock Sabbath morning. They will appreciate it and benefit from it spiritually. This kind of diligent study is encouraged by the church.[2] The pastor is paid to do this kind of work. No conscientious lawyer would dare go to court to represent his client with only one or two hours of preparation, or with someone else's brief. The man who is unprepared has to be prepared to make a fool out of himself, and also to fail as a worship leader.

The man of God must never forget that he is a man.[3] He is a man of this world. He lives in the same world as his people. The message he preaches, therefore, must be a timely message. For the Word of God to be timeless does not mean it is irrelevant. The truth never changes, but it is always truth related to life. The truth that God loved the world would not have meant much if He had not incarnated that truth in sending His Son to the world. The timeless truth became timely in the

[2]*Manual for Church Officers*, p. 47.

[3]C. Raymond Holmes, *It's a Two-Way Street* (Washington: Review and Herald Publishing Association, 1978), pp. 14–17.

incarnation. That relationship between Word and world must be communicated by the faithful preacher. Life is the context in which worship and preaching take place. Such preaching bridges the gap between doctrines as a science or discipline, and life as it is really lived. In my early ministry I found myself concentrating on the idea that my principal function in preaching was to pass on to my people the priceless gems of timeless truths I found in Scripture. Then I began to notice perplexed looks and discovered that my verbal gems had missed the congregation's hearts and heads. They were truth, yes, but unrelated to life. I was preaching theology all by itself, answering questions my congregation was not asking. Slowly, over the years, I began to realize that my task was to formulate, not just God's answers, but also my people's questions. So, for me, preaching first raises the questions that doctrine and life ask of each other, then seeks the answers to those questions in the Word of God and frames them in the contemporary words of human language.

If preaching is to be timeless the preacher must diligently study the Word of God. If it is to be timely he must also be a student of life. He cannot isolate himself from what is going on in his world and barricade himself behind a mountain of theological books. His interest in true stories about life will enliven his preaching and assist in its relevancy. The true stories of his people, told to him as he ministers pastoral care, will do the same. When it comes time for him, in his sermon preparation, to formulate his thesis, proposition, or sermon idea, it will be as true to life as it is biblically true. In fact, if it is not true to life it is not biblical, for the Bible is a book of life. The preacher is not an oracle. He is a fellow seeker charged with articulating the questions his people are asking, and with framing the answers the Bible gives.

I don't think there is such a thing as a timeless sermon. Years ago I was able to prepare a sermon, preach it to my congregation, then file it away to be used again at another time and with another congregation. But I find it increasingly more difficult to do that today. I attribute that change to a growing consciousness of my contextual responsibility as a preacher. A sermon may contain timeless truths, but it was initially prepared and preached in a particular historical context. It cannot be preached in the same way and with the same sensitivity to need in another, unfamiliar, context. A new situation demands a new sermon which reflects the context in which it is to be preached. For curiosity's sake I save all my old sermons, but I rarely preach them again. If the press of time and circumstance forces me to do it, I make an effort to contextualize that old sermon so that it can be timely again.

In my files I have a funeral sermon which I could never preach again. Even if almost identical events were to occur, it would still require contextualization. Time would have elapsed. I would have changed. The people listening would be different and living in a different time. The worshiping congregation and community would be different. It is not a timeless sermon, though the gospel it contains is certainly timeless. The tragic death of a teenage boy took place while I was away from my congregation. Upon receiving the sad news, my mind began to prepare the message I would deliver at the boy's funeral service. His mother and father and sisters hovered over my shoulder in my imagination as I prayed and thought. Also present were all the other young people in my congregation, together with his academy classmates and friends. I was expecting them all to be present at his funeral service. The sermon was timeless in that it spoke of the promise of the resurrection in relation to the uncertainty and instability of human life. But it was timely, too, as it helped frame the questions those young people were asking, some of which had no answers. Some simply had to remain questions, and the teenagers had to accept that fact and still have faith and hope.

The service itself was timely because it included a song service in which the teenagers expressed their feelings in singing together the gospel songs they loved. It included also a reading of some poetry and prose the lad had written which made it possible for him to speak vicariously to his friends. Many of them had never known the depth of soul he possessed and were deeply touched. Much reassurance was experienced by that youthful congregation that fall afternoon as multicolored rays of the sun filtered through the stained glass windows. It was a context hardly repeatable and the sermon lies buried in my files where it belongs.

The Corporate Nature of Preaching and Worship

Worship and preaching are inseparable precisely because the most profound and sublime thoughts of the human mind are those concerning God. Preaching that is truly biblical informs and forms such thoughts. Sometimes it takes a painful probing by the Word to expose how the worshiper really feels about God, his/her real concept of God. Such probing is necessary because if our concept of God is incorrect, inaccurate, incomplete, or distorted and pagan, the structure of worship will collapse and bury us under a heap of pseudo-religious rubbish.

In essence, idolatry is the insistence on maintaining ideas about God that are inconsistent with the biblical account, inconsistent with His nature as that nature is revealed by the Word. No one can worship

God rightly if he/she has not come to know Him as He is through the communication of the gospel (John 5:24; Rom 10:14–17). Worshipers need a knowledge of Him that recognizes His awesomeness and majesty, and that leads to an individual and corporate worship experience that celebrates His presence.

Worship is commanded by God. It is not an option for the Christian believer. There should never be a struggle with the question of whether or not to attend the weekly worship services appointed by the church, the body of Christ. Such worship appointments constitute an invitation from God. It is inconceivable that, apart from emergencies and circumstances beyond control, any believer should choose to absent himself when the community of faith gathers for corporate worship. This is particularly true for Seventh-day Adventist Christians, as Heb 10:25 exhorts: "Let us not give up meeting together, as some are in the habit of doing, but let us encourage one another—and all the more as you see the Day approaching" (NIV). Regular, consistent, and disciplined worship attendance ought to be habitual for Seventh-day Adventists.

Worship and preaching are intended to bring persons to the place where they bow the knee to the God of heaven in dependent praise and adoration, where the idols of life are pushed aside in favor of Him who made and redeemed the world. That will not happen without a lofty concept of God, one that draws the believer to worship not for what he/she can get out of it, but to praise the Majesty in the heavens who is present by His Spirit and through His Word. What one gets out of such worship is an added blessing, but it is not the essential goal of worship. As Revelation 4–5 so graphically portrays, worship focuses on God and His Son Jesus Christ, not on the worshiper. Such worship is Other-centered rather than self-centered.

We need the lofty and transcendent view of God represented by Ellen G. White's statement in *Testimonies*, Vol. 5, pp. 491–499.[4] She also expresses this view in the following personal experience.

> I saw the beauty and loveliness of Jesus. As I beheld His glory, the thought did not occur to me that I should ever be separated from His presence. I saw a light coming from the glory that encircled the Father, and as it approached near to me, my body trembled and shook like a leaf. I thought that if it should come near me I would be struck out of existence, but the light passed me. Then could I have some sense of the great and terrible God with whom we have to do. I saw then what faint views some have of the holiness of God, and how much they

[4]See Appendix B.

take His holy and reverend name in vain, without realizing that it is God, the great and terrible God, of whom they are speaking.[5]

We dare not surrender this lofty concept of God! Should the Seventh-day Adventist Church allow her concept of the holiness and transcendence of God to erode, she would decline along with it. As A. W. Tozer reminds us, "The first step down for any church is taken when it surrenders its high opinion of God."[6] Surrender to low views of God would destroy the very message designed to call people everywhere to worship the Majesty in the heavens rather than the devil, whose mission is to destroy mankind and the world. To lose the sense of the majesty of God is a tragedy of the greatest magnitude for a people whose very lives are dedicated to the expectation of His soon return, and who live at a time when the forces of irreligion are gathering force and momentum. If the gains of the Seventh-day Adventist Church are only external it will be in the gravest of danger. Tozer suggests, "Modern christianity is simply not producing the kind of Christian who can appreciate or experience the life in the Spirit."[7] We Adventists must not respond to this observation with smugness; instead we must ask if we are doing any better than Christianity as a whole.

The question that needs asking is not what we think about worship, but what does God think about it? not what do we get out of it, but what does God want from us? We need to think of worship primarily in terms of giving rather than in terms of getting. The hymns are sung to God, not to the congregation. The prayers are offered to God as supplication, not as a means of discovering what someone else is thinking. The anthem or special music is an offering of praise to God, not religious entertainment. And the sermon is the preacher's own offering to God as well as a means of instructing the people. That offering has been in preparation all week long. It is not cursory. It is not mediocre. It represents the best exegetical, theological, and existential thinking the preacher is capable of doing. While the communication from God to man is not limited to the best sermons, they do enhance that communication and make possible a more immediate relationship. What is required, in the words of Norval Pease, is "a balanced service, where Scripture reading, prayer, music, and preaching blend together in spiritual worship."[8]

[5]White, *Early Writings*, p. 70.

[6]A. W. Tozer, *The Knowledge of the Holy* (New York: Harper and Brothers, 1961), p. 12.

[7]Ibid., p. 6.

[8]Pease, *And Worship Him*, p. 81.

William H. Willimon rightly observes that "most of the problems which we have created throughout the history of our liturgy [worship] were the result of accentuating one aspect of worship at the expense of other aspects. Is it not the essence of heresy to cling too ardently to one facet of the truth to the exclusion of other facets of the truth? Let this be a warning to us in our pastoral concern for worship. Worship is pastoral, edifying, corporate, and integrative."[9]

Worship is not just an individual matter. The Christian has been baptized into a united body. He/she has become part of a people (1 Cor 12:1–31). Chapter 14 of 1 Corinthians indicates clearly that worship is first of all a corporate affair. According to the Word of God there are no remnant persons, only a remnant people. If a Christian community does not worship corporately, it is not a Christian community. Idolatry, therefore, consists not only of holding ideas about God that are in contradiction to Scripture, but also in holding ideas of the nature of the church and its worship that are not in harmony with the Word of God.

Which is most sacred to the one who comes to worship services, the sermon or the God who speaks through the sermon? There can be no true scriptural worship without the proclamation of the Word. Any trend that increases and elaborates liturgy and decreases and deemphasizes the sermon is dangerous and counterproductive to the church's life and mission. But by the same token the sermon is not the object of worship. The congregation gathers to celebrate the presence of God, to adore Him and praise His holy name.

One of the best statements portraying a balanced relationship between preaching and liturgy in corporate worship is found in an old homiletical classic. It reads:

> The evaluation of the sermon as an act of worship will accentuate at the same time the worship value of song and prayer and reading. The need is not more of one and less of the other but of fusing all into a harmonious worshipful whole. This does not mean that the freedom, spontaneity, simplicity, spirituality, of New Testament worship should be abandoned. The failure of many worship services to satisfy the souls of men is not because they are too simple or too free. The dissatisfaction is often caused, at least in part, by the coldness, lack of animation, want of connection, and general slovenliness which in so many cases mark our worship. We must pay far more attention to this than is common, both in the way of general cultivation and of preparation for each particular occasion. This is less necessary for those who have only to go through a form of service prepared by others than for him who,

[9]William H. Willimon, *Worship As Pastoral Care* (Nashville: Abingdon, 1979), p. 21.

on every separate occasion, is required to produce a service, for himself and for the congregation. Thoroughly simple in form, so as not to encourage the people to rest in externals, but full of interest, animation, devoutness, solemn sweetness—such should be our worship.[10]

Preaching and Church Growth

It is not my intention to discuss homiletical method in relation to church growth. What I want to do is concentrate on the preacher, who himself is an initial factor in church growth. And I want to base my remarks on the experience of Ezekiel recorded in Ezekiel 1:28b–3:4 (NIV):

> This was the appearance of the likeness of the glory of the Lord. When I saw it, I fell face down, and I heard the voice of one speaking. He said to me, "Son of man, stand up on your feet and I will speak to you." As he spoke, the Spirit came into me and raised me to my feet, and I heard him speaking to me. He said, "Son of man, I am sending you to the Israelites, to a rebellious nation that has rebelled against me; they and their fathers have been in revolt against me to this very day. The people to whom I am sending you are obstinate and stubborn. Say to them, 'This is what the sovereign Lord says.' And whether they listen or fail to listen—for they are a rebellious house—they will know that a prophet has been among them. And you, son of man, do not be afraid of them or their words. Do not be afraid, though briars and thorns are all around you and you live among scorpions. Do not be afraid of what they say or terrified by them, though they are a rebellious house. You must speak my words to them, whether they listen or fail to listen, for they are rebellious. But you, son of man, listen to what I say to you. Do not rebel like that rebellious house; open your mouth and eat what I give you." Then I looked, and I saw a hand stretched out to me. In it was a scroll, which he unrolled before me. On both sides of it were written words of lament and mourning and woe. And he said to me, "Son of man, eat what is before you, eat this scroll; then go and speak to the house of Israel." So I opened my mouth, and he gave me the scroll to eat. Then he said to me, "Son of man, eat this scroll I am giving you and fill your stomach with it." So I ate it, and it tasted as sweet as honey in my mouth. He then said to me: "Son of man, go now to the house of Israel and speak my words to them."

First, preaching for church growth requires a growing preacher, one who goes from prostration to proclamation as did Ezekiel. Before it

[10]John A. Broadus, *On the Preparation and Delivery of Sermons* (New York: Harper and Row, Publishers, 1944), p. 358.

is anything else, growth is submission. In the Christian preacher's life the prostrate position comes before the upright position. Some important things had to happen in Ezekiel's life before the Lord said, "Go to the house of Israel and speak." What preachers need, before they can even begin to do the work they have been called and equipped to do, is an experience with God like Ezekiel's! Without that, no matter how clever they are in regard to homiletical technique, their preaching will be gutless and heartless, insipid and dull. Someone has said that he has heard only three kinds of preaching: dull, duller, and dullest.

God had to prepare Ezekiel before he was ready to preach to the people. The preparation of the preacher comes before the preparation of a sermon or the preaching of it. When preachers catch a vision of God like Ezekiel's, they will respond as he did. He fell to the ground before the Lord God Almighty and didn't dare move until he was raised to his feet by the God with whom he had to do. Preaching for church growth begins with submission: utter and complete surrender before God. Why is that necessary? Does such an experience constitute a debasement of a person? Must one be humiliated like this before one can serve? The narrative does not indicate that Ezekiel felt humiliated by the experience. He did it voluntarily, yet compulsively. When God humbles His preachers it is not to humiliate them but to liberate them, to set them free from the sin that inhibits service, and to illustrate the nature of their relationship to Him. God does not make a deal with His preacher. He did not ask Ezekiel if he would do what was commanded. He does not negotiate the terms of the relationship or the job he has for the preacher to do. This is not a contract between two equals. God functions as God and simply commands and sends. Of course, the preacher is not without a choice—Ezekiel could have refused. The one called does have to respond and take the consequences of that response. But the conditions of the call are not negotiable. God does not expect or anticipate a refusal. He expects and anticipates full acceptance of the relationship and the job.

Second, preaching for growth requires a knowing preacher. He has to know the message he is to preach, understand it, accept it for himself, and live it to the fullest. He must know that the message comes from God. It is God's message, not the preacher's message. God planned it. God devised it. God composed it. He saw to its transposition into Scripture, and He imposes it on His preachers. The preacher receives it, reshapes it in contemporary language and idiom, and shares it with his people as the Word that lives again.

God told Ezekiel to say to the people, "This is what the sovereign Lord says" (vs. 4b). Also, "You must speak my words to them" (vs. 7), and, "Go now to the house of Israel and speak my words to them" (3:4). To be a preacher means to preach a message that has been given by God and received by faith. No matter what the results of the proclamation might be, it is always the given message that must be preached. No spiritual growth can take place if preachers do not preach what God has given them to preach.

That message must never be received only intellectually, only as the result of training in college religion departments or theological seminaries. As Ezekiel's experience illustrates dramatically, the message must be eaten by the preacher. He is not ready to preach to others until he has first ingested and digested the message for himself. When he has internalized the objective truth and it has become existential, part of his being and self understanding, when he has tasted the sweetness of grace and redemption and the call to service, then he has a message to give.

There is a vital relationship between the message and the messenger. To be sure, the message has validity, authority, and power in itself. In essence these are not dependent on the messenger. But if the messenger has not "eaten" the message, and, rather than preaching it, questions it and adjusts it to suit his own opinion, he will only contribute to his hearers' natural skepticism. The messenger's own attitude toward the message has much to do with its reception by others. The fact is that it is not the preacher's word but God's Word that brings about transformation of life, true conversion, and faith. God's promise to His preacher is that He will shut the preacher's mouth if His preacher does not preach His message. This is especially important in critical times, in the face of judgment and destruction.

The preacher must know the people to whom he preaches. In the modern world one must earn the right to be heard. Ezekiel understood that, and said, "I came to the exiles who lived in Tel Aviv near the Kebar River. And there, where they were living, I sat among them for seven days—overwhelmed" (3:15). Only when the preacher has done that is he able to respond to preaching texts as a total self. Preaching for growth requires that the preaching text be interpreted in terms of human existence. One must not be satisfied with answers to the questions: "What is the text saying?", "What is the doctrinal truth here?", but must also ask: "To what human problem, need, or issue does the text address itself?", "What does this mean for my life?", and, "How does the text help me find personal fulfillment and wholeness?" This hermeneutical task is possible when the preacher realizes that the biblical text confronts a person on more than one level of awareness. People who listen to such preachers will ask, "How does our pastor know so well what we are thinking and experiencing?" The answer, of course, is that he sits among them and does not address them from the safety of an ivory tower. The sermons preached by this kind of preacher have the possibility of constituting help in themselves.

Third, preaching for church growth requires fearless preachers. Without having responded to God in prostration, without that submission, Ezekiel would have been hard put to preach to the kind of people the Lord described. There are usually two fears connected with the call to ministry: the fear of failure and the fear of success. I have often been afraid I could not do the job He called me to do because I did not feel qualified or gifted for it. But He calls anyway. And one is pulled into it as steel is pulled to a magnet. It is only the kind of submission exhibited by Ezekiel that makes ministry possible in the face of the overwhelming challenges to ministry presented by contemporary life, society, confusion respecting doctrinal issues, and personal inadequacies felt by the minister.

I have also been fearful of success in ministry, because I had the impression that if I did my job well it would get me into trouble. The better I became at it the more trouble I could expect. That's enough to scare the ministry out of anyone. What a catalogue of woe is found in 2 Cor 6:4–10 where Paul speaks of his ministry in fearful terms: " . . . in much endurance, in affliction, in hardships, in distress, in beatings, in imprisonments, in tumults, in labors, in sleeplessness, in hunger . . . by glory and dishonor, by evil report and good report; regarded as deceivers and yet true; as unknown yet well-known; as dying yet behold, we live; as punished yet not put to death; as sorrowful yet always rejoicing; as poor yet making many rich; as having nothing yet possessing all things." What person in his right mind would want to get involved in such work when faithfulness and professional excellence are rewarded with such things? What a job description! After all, everyone has a natural desire to be accepted and appreciated and loved. Who wants resistance, opposition, even persecution as the rewards of obedience? But that's what ministry is all about. God does not lie. He told Ezekiel the truth.

But preaching is also a sublime vocation. The afflicted are not crushed; the perplexed do not despair; the persecuted are not forsaken; those struck down are not destroyed. Rather, the very life of Jesus is manifested in them. So, whether people will listen to the Word of God or not, preachers must preach it fearlessly.

Fourth, to preach for church growth requires a faithful preacher. "But you, son of man, listen to what I say *to you.* Do not rebel like that rebellious house; open your mouth and eat what I give you" (vs. 8).

That element of the prophetic office which has been identified as "forthtelling" is essential to the Adventist preaching ministry. There is no need to apologize for our message, His message, the message that converts people to Jesus Christ and prepares them for His return. A prophet must be faithful to message and mission. He/she is dedicated and careful to transmit the message God has given. That's why there are so few prophets. There are many preachers and theologians, but God wants His workers to first be prophets, then theologians and preachers. "The prophet is the chosen means whereby God intervenes in the affairs of men. The whole of history demonstrates this, not only that of the people of Israel. And not only in religious matters but also in politics, economy, law, and social organization. Our hope today in this crisis of our civilization is that God will send us prophets, speaking clearly and without any taint of compromise with power."[11]

But there are few who are ready and willing to pay the price, who are willing to give up their lives for the job. Many are willing to give up their jobs for the sake of their lives, but how many are willing to give up their lives for the sake of the job to which God calls? The fact is there is no growth without pain. Preachers must be willing, like Paul, to suffer whatever is required of them for the sake of fulfilling their ministry.

Without the experience described in chapter 2, Ezekiel would never have done what is described in chapter 37. There the preacher who received the message preached the message. The results were dramatic. The dead were given life! Not because the preacher preached, but because he preached what God gave him to preach. Without that transaction the dead will not be made alive, for life comes only by the Word of God. Preachers do not convert sinners and revive saints. Only God does that by means of His Word. It is only the submissive preacher who has heard the Word and internalized the Word who will preach the Word come what may. Without such preachers and such preaching there could be no real church growth, no increase in the body of worshipers.

Pastoral Preaching

The Seventh-day Adventist Church has two major goals. One is evangelistic and the other is pastoral. The evangelistic goal is salvation, to win the world for Christ. The pastoral goal is sanctification, to win the church to holy living. The first has to do with quantitative growth,

[11]Paul Tournier, *The Violence Within* (San Francisco: Harper and Row, Publishers, 1978), p. 184.

the second with qualitative growth. The first is initiation into the faith, the second is preparation for witness and for the glorified life after the resurrection. The first goal concerns birth, the beginning of the Christian life; the second goal concerns growth toward the culmination of that life. Evangelistic preaching is used by the Holy Spirit to help people become Christians. Pastoral preaching is used by the Holy Spirit to help Christians live faithfully and by so doing become truly human.

Preaching must be carefully balanced between these twin goals. To train every minister to be only an evangelist would be a mistake, and would constitute a misunderstanding of the spiritual gifts. Some are called to be evangelists, and some pastors. Not all are pastors, and not all are evangelists. Finishing the work of God cannot be done solely in terms of evangelism. There is also the building up of the body of Christ in the faith. That is a pastoral concern, and pastors as well as evangelists are gifts of the Spirit to the church (Eph 4:11).

Worship, in which the Word of God is ministered to the saints, is the basic context in which such building up takes place. The gifts of the Spirit are for the purpose that "the body of Christ may be built up . . . and become mature" (Eph 4:12–13, NIV). Therefore, what is needed is a proper balance between a pulpit-centered and an action-centered worship service. When the entire burden for the success of a worship service is placed on the minister's shoulders, as is the case in the free church tradition, the conception of worship as a form of religious entertainment is fostered. Consequently concern for liturgical integrity and for some knowledge of the importance music and hymnology play in worship is met with confusion and blank stares, as though an unmentionable had been mentioned.

Is leading in worship one of the major tasks of the Seventh-day Adventist minister? In the light of what has been said so far in this book, the answer should be obvious. Pastors need to take worship leadership seriously, as seriously as does the *Manual for Church Officers:* "The Sabbath services are among the most important occasions that arise during a week. They afford precious opportunities for Bible study, fellowhsip, and worship, and everything possible should be done to make these services as attractive and helpful as possible. . . . The pastor is primarily responsible for the way these services are conducted."[12]

It is within the context of the Sabbath services that preaching can be specifically pastoral. The flow of pastoral ministry goes from worship to calling on the members, from preaching to counseling. Public

[12]*Manual for Church Officers*, p. 53.

ministry leads to private ministry, and private ministry revitalizes and informs public ministry. Good pastoral preaching will lead to counseling, and the insights gained in counseling will help the pastor to deal with the crucial issues of life in his sermons. In fact, pastoral preaching can be compared to preventive medicine. Many potential problems in the lives of the members can be averted, exposed for help, and even resolved through the preaching of a sensitive and alert pastor. Such preaching can be therapeutic and healing in itself.

Many preachers make the asumption that to expound a biblical text assures relevancy. But it is not enough to deal with questions concerning the original meaning of a biblical text. The text must be dealt with existentially as well. Its meaning for today must be adequately explored if the sermon is to result in inner change and spiritual growth for its hearers. Too many sermons come too late to do any good because they are out of touch with life as it is lived.

Preaching is not primarily a theological or a liturgical activity. It is first and foremost a pastoral activity. Worship, in which the public proclamation of the Word occurs, will not assume the prominent place it should have for Seventh-day Adventists until it can be seen both pastorally and evangelistically by pastors and lay members alike.

Pastoral preaching is characterized as "active compassion" by Gary D. Stratman.[13] The pastor is not one who talks about compassion. The pastor is compassionate. Pastoral preaching is done by a person who cares. It is out of such compassion that the pastor speaks prophetically, biblically, in terms of redemption and judgment. When sin is exposed and calls for repentance are made, it is because the pastor cannot bear to think of any church member being lost eternally for want of forgiveness and grace.

The pastoral preacher knows that it is harder to maintain faith than to attain it. The struggle to stay in the faith at times is far greater than the struggle to become a believer. Furthermore, bringing the work of God to its completion in the hearts of the people requires Paul's counsel to young pastor Timothy: "Preach the Word; be prepared in season and out of season; correct, rebuke and encourage—with great patience" (2 Tim 4:2, NIV). It takes real love to do that. It takes a pastor who is concerned about the eternal welfare of his people above concern for his own popularity and prestige. With respect to such pastoral preaching Ellen White wrote:

> Some enter the ministry without a deep love to God or to their fellow men. Selfishness and self-indulgence will be manifested in the lives of

[13]Gary D. Stratman, *Pastoral Preaching* (Nashville: Abingdon, 1983), p. 31.

> such; and while these unconsecrated, unfaithful watchmen are serving themselves instead of feeding the flock and attending to their pastoral duties, the people perish for want of proper instruction.
>
> In every discourse fervent appeals should be made to the people to forsake their sins and turn to Christ. The popular sins and indulgences of the day should be condemned and practical godliness enforced. The minister should be deeply in earnest himself, feeling from the heart the words he utters and unable to repress his feeling of concern for the souls of men and women for whom Christ has died.[14]

It is obvious that the pastor of whom she speaks is a caring person, whose ministry reflects the pastoral dimension C. W. Brister describes:

> A preacher is addressing his congregation pastorally when he carries the burden of the Lord and of man into the dialogue of the sanctuary. His objective is to drive a shaft of healing light into the cancerous tissues of human existence. He becomes a spiritual mentor of men precisely when burdens are lifted, guilt is relieved, high purposes are forged, and hope is rekindled in the human heart. On a larger scale, he may try to turn the tide in the life of a congregation that has lost its way—become listless or introverted or indifferent about life's great issues. For example, in an effort to stir his church to new devotion one minister delivered a course of doctrinal sermons on the church—its origins, nature, true head, ministry, and message. Under the general theme of "The Fellowship of Confession," his sermons reflected profound pastoral intent. What then is the content of pastoral preaching to be? Nothing less than the Word of God! It is precisely of thin, superficial sermons that laymen are weary. . . . [T]he interpreter of the Word has a great responsibility to God and to his people. He must not misrepresent the divine-human situation through superficial utterances and misuse of sacred symbols. Preachers prostitute religion to unworthy purposes who offer God as an antidote to anxiety or as a sure source of strength to obtain personal success in the secular order. God's Word comes as a gift, but also as a claim upon men's lives, requiring obedience. The servant of the Word is to be a man of the people, a man of the Book, and a man of God. Without God's presence in his life the preacher has nothing of ultimate worth to offer those who hear his words. Jesus reminded His disciples, "Apart from me you can do nothing" (John 15:5). A pastoral preacher who would lead others to sense the presence of God must be at home in the divine presence himself.[15]

Pastoral preaching is essential because God's work must be finished in the inner being, as well as in the larger context of the world. It

[14]White, *Testimonies for the Church*, Vol. 4, p. 396.

[15]C. W. Brister, *Pastoral Care in the Church* (New York: Harper and Row Publishers, 1964), pp. 116–117.

is essential because the members of the church are always, until Jesus comes again, threatened with the loss of the sacred. Thus in truly pastoral preaching there must be a careful balance between sensitivity to human need and sensitivity to the Word of God. Human needs are to be met by God's Word. But sometimes the need is the problem. For example, the need to "do one's own thing" may require a call for repentance so that the deeper need for faith and obedience can be met, so that the believer can "do God's thing" instead. It means telling the truth about the truth, daring to be radically biblical, subjecting all thought and all life to the intense and revealing scrutiny of the Word of God.

Pastoral preaching does not necessarily begin with the presentation of a life-situation problem requiring resolution. Homiletical method is not the key. Pastoral preaching occurs when the preacher consistently uses Bible texts "that allow comfort, demand, strength and judgment to speak from within the *full* biblical witness."[16] The preacher who desires to preach pastorally will wrestle with the biblical text and with the needs of his people, but never without personal involvement and pain. He/she is always one who cares and cares profoundly, one who in his/her care models the care of God.

It must be remembered, however, that in the context of worship other parts of the service may be more pastoral in nature than the sermon. Thank God this is so, for there are preachers who do not care. In such cases the care of God comes through in other ways. It may be that the only gospel heard during the Sabbath service will come by means of Scripture readings, hymn singing, the sacraments, or even prayers. The liturgical action may be more pastorally proclamatory than the sermon itself. Therefore, the rest of the order of service requires as diligent attention as does the preparation and preaching of the sermon. Other elements in the service may meet the congregation's need to praise, to confess, to hear the Word of forgiveness. The very liturgy itself can often provide a response to loneliness and isolation, or even grief, as the believer shares in the whole congregation's focus on God and the Son in praise and petition and joy unspeakable.

It is unfortunate, but there tends to be the feeling that evangelistic and pastoral preaching are competitive and are therefore mutually exclusive. The truth is, in view of the twin goals mentioned above, that God's work will not be finished any faster one way than another. In order to build a building certain materials are required. The conversion of clay into bricks, cement into blocks, and iron into steel provides

[16]Stratman, *Pastoral Preaching*, p. 16.

the material. That's what evangelism does. But that is not the actual construction. Construction is accomplished when the materials are arranged in a new way according to a plan which shapes the building for its use. The function of pastoring is to build the church with the materials provided by evangelism (see Ephesians 2–4).

I once heard a respected churchman say, "We should not have to hear a sermon on Sabbath. Preachers should be out evangelizing." One is prompted to ask what the church members will be doing while the pastor is out evangelizing. He had forgotten, or had never known, that the church and its members need to be reborn weekly. That's the purpose of the Sabbath: not only to remember that God once created, but to experience again the recreative power of the same creative Word shared in worship.

Discussion Questions

1. Is it correct to speak of worship as the "preaching service"?
2. What is the biblical, theological, historical rationale for the centrality of preaching in SDA worship?
3. What form should ministerial accountability take with respect to the preaching process?
4. Does a person's, or a church's, concept of God have any relation to attitudes concerning corporate worship and worship attendance?
5. How can we assure that preaching is balanced between the evangelistic and pastoral goals of the SDA Church?

Worship and Evangelism / 12

In the city of Berlin, Germany, in 1966, the first World Congress on Evangelism was held. It attracted more than 1200 delegates from over 100 countries. The report of the Congress consisted of two volumes containing various papers that were presented, reports on evangelistic techniques used in various parts of the world, and discussion summaries. Not once in 846 pages was anything said concerning the relationship between the worship of the church and its evangelistic task. That could hardly be an oversight. No doubt the omission reflects a widespread, and to a certain degree legitimate, belief that in its evangelistic thrust the church manifests its essential nature and primary task in the world.[1] But evangelism must always be firmly rooted in the soil of the church's worship and liturgical life.

Evangelism as the Extension of Worship

The Mennonite scholar Myron Augsburger, in his excellent little book on evangelism, *Invitation to Discipleship*, begins with the statement, "Evangelism is the life of the Church."[2] To speak of life is to speak about power, about the source of power, not necessarily about activity. The *life*, the *heartbeat*, of the church is worship. Evangelism is the consequence, the natural and powerful outgrowth or result, of

[1]In the book *Evangelism in the Early Church* by Michael Green (Grand Rapids, Mich.: Eerdmans, 1970), worship is not mentioned in the subject index. It is hard to believe that the evangelistic thrust of early Christianity was unrelated to the worship life of the early church!

[2]Myron Augsburger, *Invitation to Discipleship* (Scottdale, Pa.: Herald Press, 1967), p. 1.

the church's worship life. It is the expression of the church's worship extended into the world.

There is no question but that the New Testament church was committed to evangelism. It is the mission of the church to save souls. She cannot keep her faith to herself and still be the church. Her life is two-dimensional. Jesus first said, "Come to me," and then He said, "Go into all the world." There is no going without coming. "Come" comes before "go." Far too many church members have the idea that once one comes and then goes he need not come anymore, that all of his energies and intentions must now be devoted to winning the lost. Consequently, for them, worship becomes a bore and every worship service must take the form of an evangelistic meeting with an altar call or it is judged to be worthless and even apostate.

The church is not just the body of people that raises the money for evangelism. Our interest and involvement in worship must go far beyond the idea that it is the gathered church that generates the funds for evangelism. Too often we hear thoughtless criticism of the money the church spends for its worship centers, saying it should be spent for evangelism instead. But there is the possibility that a lot of money could be wasted in evangelism simply because the supply is unlimited. Funds for evangelism are always available. However, to build a church building requires scraping the bottom of the barrel for funds.

What do we do with the souls that are saved? How do we keep them in the church? All the worship they have known has been the theatricality and emotion of evangelistic meetings; they have never known the joy, the aesthetic thrill to be found in the fellowship of a congregation engaged in regular weekly worship in its own sanctuary. These new converts need to become part of the worshiping body of believers each week. Incorporating new believers into the body of Christ is part of the church's evangelistic mission. I agree with Hoon's statement: "The Church's missionary power is in ratio to her liturgical integrity."[3] Worship that leads to mission is not self-centered and individualistic. It is corporate worship that is truly missionary and evangelistic in nature.

The church has been called into being for its own sake and for the sake of the world. The church is the fellowship of believers who need the strength of fellowship and the encouragement that comes from corporate worship so they can learn to be Christian in the world. God has created the church to give glory and praise to Him. Its first work is to worship God and lift Him up before the eyes of all people everywhere.

[3]Hoon, *The Integrity of Worship*, p. 59.

The World Is Aware of the Church's Worship

The church was not created solely for God, however; it was also created for the world. It is only when the church understands and appreciates its call to worship that it can understand and appreciate its call to evangelize. When the church gathers for worship, the world is there too. In the gathering of the church it becomes apparent to the world that there is a people of God in its midst. It is among the people of the world that the people of God are to live. The corporate body of Christ, by means of its individual members, must permeate society and culture in righteous and holy living. This is living evangelistically. In that sense the gathered church is scattered into the world.

As witness and observer, then, the world participates in the praise and worship of the church. This too is a sort of foretaste of the final praise the entire world will give to the Lord in the kingdom. It is because God wants as many as possible to be in that number that the church does evangelism. The outcome of the seven last plagues will be the singing of the song of Moses: "Great and marvelous are thy works O Lord God the almighty, righteous and true are Thy ways, Thou King of the nations; Who will not fear O Lord and glorify Thy name? For Thou alone art holy; for all the nations will come and worship before Thee" (Rev 15:3–4).

The worship of the church constitutes an invitation to the world to come and join in that worship. Yes, the gathering of the church may often be an offense to the world. The church in worship is a reminder to the world of its true condition, of its apostasy and rebellion, of its waywardness. The worship of the church is intended to prick the conscience of the world and remind it of the judgment that is to come and of the coming of the Saviour and Lord. The life of the church is different from that of the world, so it will always be an offense as long as mankind lives in sin and rebellion. But that very difference constitutes an invitation to come and join the group whose goals and values are so radically different from the world's.

Only the church can lead the world in worship because only the church is made up of the redeemed whose lives have been reoriented by divine grace. They alone can direct the world's attention to the will and purpose of God. It is *in* the world, and as part of the world's time and space, that the church worships. The church building is built in the world's space and is, therefore, an intrusion, just as God Himself intrudes into man's life. The Sabbath day, while sanctified by the will and command of God, is also a part of the world's time. The world is misusing that time, and the Sabbath, as the time when the church becomes visible, is a constant reminder to the world of its waywardness and sin. That is why the Sabbath as opposed to Sunday is such an offense to many. The Sabbath is a reminder to all of Christendom that there is more growth for believers and for the Christian church as a whole.

The Worshiping Church Is Aware of the World

On the other side of the picture is the fact that as the faithful gather for worship the world becomes known to the church. As the church worships it is conscious of the world in which it must live and which is observing and sometimes intruding on the church's worship life. The world cannot escape the church, and the church cannot escape the world. The very existence of the church is for the sake of those who do not belong to it. The church is *always* a missionary community. Not to understand this and feel this and sense this is to miss entirely the reality of the church and to misunderstand the nature of its life in the world as well as the nature of its worship. One cannot sing hymns, hear sermons, celebrate the Lord's Supper, and baptize new members without being acutely aware of the world outside the door. Worship is the most conspicuous activity of the church because it occurs on a regular basis on a special day. Evangelism may be more spectacular, but worship is more conspicuous.

Worship Leads to Mission

The Sabbath reminds the church that it is still in the world in that it has been granted one special day out of seven for its worship and devotional life. The Sabbath also demonstrates to the world that the church is in its midst, and that in God's economy six days are for work and the seventh is the Lord's special day on which He is to be honored and praised. It is in its worship that the church becomes aware of itself as an apostolic community with a call and responsibility to preach the gospel in all the world. In worship the church is profoundly expressing its love for the world.

Let us return to Hoon's statement that "the Church's missionary power is in ratio to her liturgical integrity." Liturgical integrity has to do first with what the church does when it worships, and second with its attitude toward what it does. If the church's worship life is not important enough to give it the theological/liturgical attention it deserves, what purpose is gained by inviting others to join its fellowship? My plea is that we think of worship in terms of what Hoon calls "theological truthfulness."[4] That is to say, we must make our worship

[4]Hoon, *The Integrity of Worship*, p. 59.

services representative of what we believe. We must rid ourselves of liturgical ambiguity so that we can make a clear liturgical statement every Sabbath. Part of that statement is the clear note that the church is scattered, sent, into all the world for the next six days and that it has an evangelistic responsibility there during those six days. This responsibility includes accepting those six days' demands in terms of Christian commitment, sacrifice, and even suffering if it is required. During those six days the church must give itself to the world as its Lord gave Himself to the world and continues to give Himself in and through the church. The six days are for work, the work of witness and evangelism.

The six days are not just to live through, to put up with reluctantly until the Sabbath comes again when the world can be ignored. One day is for the Lord. He is not selfish. Six days are for the world. The Sabbath is celebrated *in* the world. In its gathering for worship, the church is preparing itself for the scattering. That is evangelism *and* liturgical integrity. It is also theological truthfulness, which means that in our liturgy we clearly portray, illustrate, define, and express what we believe. This is the only way the world can know who and what the church is. And we are reminded too, over and over again, of what we are as the church. This is the way persons of the world and members of the church are challenged by the gospel's requirements. In the former case the gospel challenge is for redemption, and in the latter case the gospel challenge is for evangelistic living.

"Authentic worship," says Hoon, "if we only realized it, is one of the most powerful forms of mission and evangelism the Church can employ."[5] It is obvious that authentic worship is that which is most illustrative of our theology on the one hand, and most concerned about the condition of the world on the other. It is worship in its most beautiful form and expression, but it is not worship isolated from the reality of life in the world. If the church is going to be the evangelistic agent God intends it to be, then it must constantly repeat to itself the message of Jesus Christ. It is to that message that the church must remain faithful, and it is motivated to faithfulness by what it hears in preaching and sees liturgically dramatized. Without worship there can be no real evangelism, and without evangelism worship fails in its purposes.

Liturgical integrity also means that the message we hear must not be reduced to secular humanism and its system of values. When we worship we do not only celebrate life, as some liturgiologists would say today. We celebrate the acts of God in history. We celebrate what He has done and is doing. The liturgy of the church must be rooted in those

[5]Hoon, *The Integrity of Worship*, p. 59.

revelatory events that are salvific. Worship is the recognition of the supreme worth of God, not the supreme worth of man. The Sabbath reminds us that God the Father and God the Son are the center of our worship, not man and his world. The preoccupation with the secular today has made its impact even on the church of the last days. When the worship of the church is man-centered we can expect all sorts of eccentricities to appear. This has been particularly true with music and instrumentation. The dramatic intervention of God in history in the incarnation, the grace and mercy revealed in the cross of Christ and His resurrection, and the obedience God demands from His creatures are all displaced in a man-centered liturgy. This is certainly not the kind of worship depicted in Rev 4–5.

The ministry of Jesus in the heavenly sanctuary is in terms of service to mankind. This is reflected in His great liturgical prayer recorded in John 17. The Christ-event was for the world. The ministry of Christ in heaven is for the world. The church which is invited to "come to me" is told to "go into all the world." In offering herself to Christ in worship the church offers herself to the world in service. As God so loved the world and gave His only Son in sacrificial service, so His church is to love the world and give itself.

It is the very life of the church lived out evangelistically that is offered for the world each day. This is especially dramatized and proclaimed in the Lord's Supper which includes the ordinance of footwashing. Gathering leads to scattering. The same steps that lead into the sanctuary on the Sabbath take the believer out again into the world when the worship service has ended. The visible church again becomes invisible and permeates society with its influence and the love of its Lord who loves the world. Evangelism is actually the extension of the church's worship into the world as the people of God become the true sacrament, broken bread and poured-out wine in sacrificial service.

Christian worship does not end when the benediction is pronounced. It continues in the form of service in the world. That which the church has been prepared to do during its Sabbath activities it now offers itself to do for the next six days. It is the worshiping church that reaches beyond itself into the world of fallen mankind to offer the gospel that has given it life. The church's worship must bear fruit, share itself abroad, pour itself out. The gospel which gives the church its life causes it to spend its life, to give its life. Sabbath is given for the world. The heavenly ministry of Christ is for the world. The second advent of Christ is for the world. Worship and evangelism are both rooted in these three revelations of divine grace as they represent the three time dimensions of man's earthbound existence.

Worship obliges the church to send forth evangelists and missionaries. From the assembly of the Sabbath comes the mission of the church. That's why Dr. Pease began his book with the statement, "The success of the Church to which we are devoting our lives depends to a great extent on what happens between eleven and twelve o'clock on Sabbath mornings."[6] It is during the Sabbath hours, particularly in worship and study, that the church learns the new song and how to sing it effectively among the people of the world.

Discussion Questions

1. What is the relationship between worship and evangelism? Are they synonymous?
2. What significance does the worship of the church have for the world?
3. Is there any relationship between the seventh-day Sabbath, the six work days, and worship and evangelism?

[6]Pease, *And Worship Him*, p. 7.

Worship and Culture / 13

Studies in anthropology have shown that the beliefs and rituals of many modern peoples reflect the beliefs and rituals found in ancient cultures. This phenomenon may result not so much from religious evolution as from the influence of an existing cultural tradition upon an emerging one. Religion for primitive man was a part of daily life rather than a separate entity. Events were explained in terms of action by invisible forces rather than by natural causes. Primitive man viewed himself and his world in religious terms and expressed his understanding in ceremonial rites. Modern man compartmentalizes his existence, often relegating religion to the periphery if it is present at all. The modern makes a distinction between the material and the spiritual. Consequently other rituals, such as those connected with work, play, family, and nation, take the place of the religious. A distinction between sacred and secular is made by moderns which would have been unthinkable to the primitive. For him religion was spontaneous, and so were rituals. Religion was also more social than individualistic, more corporate and community-centered than private.

Cultural Significance of Ritual

Some anthropologists hold that the best way to study primitive religion is to analyze rituals, because rituals portray the basic beliefs of peoples. Sacrifice, communion, atonement, and reconciliation are all religious ideas common among primitives and acted out ceremonially. Holiness is a primitive idea expressed in the setting apart of a sacred place for the reenactment of ritual. Things, places, and persons are set aside for service to the deity, oftentimes with elaborate rites. Rules of ritual observance are circumscribed and meticulously observed.

These ideas and actions also appear in the ancient Hebrew religion. Its rituals reveal its beliefs. While ritual changed among the Hebrews during the different periods of their history, it did not die out. Rather a uniformity of ritual beliefs developed, climaxing in the sanctuary services, particularly those having to do with atonement. These rituals provide the key to understanding Hebrew theology. There is simply no way to discover fully the theological meaning of atonement in the Old or New Testaments apart from a careful study of the atonement rituals of the ancient Hebrews. In such study the relationship between belief and ritual depiction becomes obvious.

The development of rituals to illustrate beliefs did not end with the Old Testament. It has continued in the formulation of Christian concepts and doctrines and subsequent liturgical expression. The same fundamental Hebraic religious ideas are found in Christian beliefs, but the rituals that express those ideas have changed. The idea of atonement now has its focus in Jesus Christ rather than in the animal sacrifices of the Old Testament. The idea of communion focuses on the Lord's Supper ritual rather than on the ritual of the Passover meal. Reconciliation is made possible by the shedding of Christ's blood rather than that of animals and is ritualized in the drinking of communion wine. The Christian ritual of inclusion, baptism, has taken the place of the Hebrew rite of circumcision. The basic ideas remain the same but with a new focus, understanding, and fulfillment that is Christian. It was a natural development that Christian rituals should take on a new form expressive of this new focus and understanding.

If the most productive way to communicate the Christian faith in non-Christian cultures is by searching for redemptive analogies and giving them Christian interpretation and meaning, it would seem the same should be true when it comes to ritual. Rituals already established as part of a culture may be retained and given a Christian significance. Of course, not all cultural rituals can be so reinterpreted if they retain a firmly established pagan or non-Christian meaning that inhibits clear communication. Consequently a thorough cultural knowledge is required for the modern missionary. He must be able to discern redemptive analogies which do lend themselves to Christian interpretation and ritual reenactment. The ancient Hebrews were certainly not influenced by every religious idea and every rite of the cultures which surrounded them. It stands to reason, however, that a cultural element containing a redemptive analogy ought also to have ritual elements which could be utilized to illustrate Christian meaning. When existing ritual is explained in Christian terms, understanding and a more ready acceptance of Christian truth result.

The point is that whether ritual be primitive or modern, pagan or Christian, it fulfills the same purpose: as creative drama it actualizes the hopes of those participating. The Adventist congregation that sings the benedictory response suggested in Appendix A senses anew the hope it corporately shares. The singing is an uplifting, reaffirming experience. What is proclaimed and illustrated liturgically actually happens: the participants become hopeful. "We Have This Hope" fixes their thought, their inner eyes, their consciousness, on the Lord's imminent return. The belief becomes "visible" in liturgical action. This is not a magical occurrence, because it is knowledge of the Advent doctrine and faith in its validity and fulfillment that form the basis of the liturgical drama. The important thing is what the congregation believes when it participates in ritual. It is the belief that gives meaning to the ritual, while at the same time the ritual dramatizes and reinforces the belief. This is precisely the reason why ritual alone, unrelated to underlying truth, is meaningless and dangerous. It is also the reason why religious truth, which by its very nature demands ritual expression, must give rise to the right kind of ritual.

Adventist Subculture and Ritual

Seventh-day Adventists interpret life and spirituality from within their own subculture as well as from within a particular national culture. This has both positive and negative consequences. Positively it makes possible the building of a very strong community of faith in which members share a common dedication and cause to which they give utmost loyalty and support. It contributes toward the inculcation and maintenance of purity of doctrine and of faith. Negatively, this uniform subculture can serve to inhibit an understanding of the positive role all culture plays in human life and in the development of religion and its traditions. The positive elements in other Christian traditions, as well as those of different cultures, can be overlooked. A sort of inner-directed and suspicious perspective can emerge which inhibits relationships and communication. Concern for purity of faith and doctrine, while good and necessary, can sometimes insulate people from the good in other faiths. Consequently there may be an unwillingness to learn from others or to believe that God is at work in other churches, other faiths, and other cultures.

To be sure, there is always the danger of perversion in worship by too much cultural assimilation. This is just as true in Europe and America as anywhere else in the world. The problem is the difficulty of separating our understanding of worship from the influence of our own culture. To say it another way, in America we have perhaps unconsciously equated the substance of the Christian faith with the culture we represent. We conclude, for example, that what is American is Christian and what is Christian is American. It may not be possible for an individual to divorce his understanding of the faith from his own culture. After all, Christianity has always come to every person wrapped in a cultural package. However, awareness of the problems that fact creates for missions and communication ought to make us open and sympathetic to the situation among Christians in cultures other than our own.

Belief, Ritual, and the Cultural Package

Americanism and worship are often indistinguishable. Most missionaries have come to the Eastern part of the world from Europe or America. Thus there has been a Westernizing and/or Americanizing of church life along with the Christianizing of peoples. Seventh-day Adventist church services in the Far East, for example, are often similar to those of the upper Midwest in the United States. It makes little difference whether one worships in the Pasay SDA Church in Manila or the Pioneer Memorial SDA Church in Berrien Springs, Michigan. The worship rituals are similar. In most cases the Far Eastern service is a direct transplantation of American Adventist form and liturgy. At the same time that our evangelization was successful, the Westernization of the church was also successful.

But Christians are not the only ones who have made, and are making, this mistake. The same mistake is being made today by non-Christian religious movements such as the International Society for Krishna Consciousness, or Hare Krishna. In this Oriental religious movement making inroads in the United States, devotees meet weekly to discuss the philosophy and meaning of Krishna in the midst of a celebration of Indian foods. They too, apparently, find it difficult to separate what they believe from the cultural package in which it comes. Indian food is served at Hare Krishna celebrations in America, while American hymns are sung at worship services by Christian congregations in India. It would be difficult for a Hare Krishna advocate to think of making his neighborhood evangelistic visits dressed in a pair of American Levis and old tennis shoes rather than a saffron robe, shaved head, and white stripes painted on his face. It is evidently not thought possible to communicate Hare Krishna beliefs without the beating of an Indian drum and the tinkling of finger cymbals. Christianity probably has an advantage in that its ideas have validity apart from culture and will survive in any case. That, of course, is one of the best arguments for contextualization: it demonstrates the universal validity of Christian truth. By contrast, Hare Krishna in Levis, eating hamburgers and drinking Coke, would be hard put to survive in America on its beliefs alone.

Revivalism is the theological and ritual tradition the Seventh-day Adventist Church has inherited from its cultural origins on the East Coast and from midwestern America during the late nineteenth and early twentieth centuries. In revivalism the goal of worship was conversion. The Methodist Church, the Reformed Churches, and the Free Churches were most affected by revivalism during these decades. The Roman Catholic, Lutheran, and Anglican communions were least affected, due, among other reasons, to a solidified liturgical tradition. Worship in these latter churches did not take on an evangelistic character. That period of American history had a major cultural influence on the emerging and developing Adventist theology and worship. Certainly it was a watershed period in the history of the world and of Christian thought, but the Adventist Church did not come into being in a historical vacuum. It clearly reflects today, everywhere it is found in the world, the cultural context of its origin.

Many American churches in the period, and later, rejected revivalism. The Seventh-day Adventist Church did not. It was born in revival. It was a part of that ethos and that climate. It was fostered and nurtured in that cultural milieu. God used the history of that period to help the emerging new church assimilate and retain an important emphasis in its life and witness.

However, revivalism overemphasized can have a negative effect on pastoral work. Evangelistic passion can override concern for the nurture of the new convert, resulting in weak members and weak congregations, to say nothing of the loss of discouraged members. There is always a pressing need for pastoral work among newly baptized Adventists. They need the attention and nurture of their pastors so they can become strong witnesses in their communities and in their extended families. The moral, ethical, social, and religious implications of the gospel must be carefully taught to them. They need to learn and experience the meanings, joys, and values of Christian fellowship and corporate worship, as well as the importance of sacrificial giving and service. An emphasis which stops at conversion, as revivalism frequently does, does not meet these needs.

Yet within revivalism there are many positive elements which must be preserved, and which have emerged again as a result of the recent liturgical revival. Spontaneity, the need to address the listener contextually, a people-centered approach, and an appreciation for the unsophisticated expression of church music are some of those positive elements. As Seventh-day Adventists we are concerned with refinement as opposed to the ecstatic, but always in the context of informality and spontaneity. To be refined does not mean to be staid, unmoving, rigid, unbending, and old-fashioned.

In the early twentieth century many American churches began to move away from revivalism toward the aesthetic in worship. Seventh-day Adventists are just now beginning to participate in that swing. In itself it is a good thing, as it reflects concern for the participation of the whole person in worship. But it must not be allowed to go too far, to the point where the positive elements of revivalism are forgotten for the sake of sophistication. Conflict is often experienced between pastors and church musicians in this respect. The church musician, and rightly so, is concerned about the aesthetic and the best in sacred music, while the pastor, based on more personal contact with his members, understands their lack of sophistication. To meet the needs of people, there will always be a place for the revivalistic, subjective, gospel song in modern SDA church worship. That does not rule out aesthetic values and appreciation of a more developed, intellectual type of music. It does mean, however, that we must be sympathetic and understanding when it comes to people's feelings and opinions about music and religious art.

Cultural Contextualizing of Worship

Often the Westerner who is sensitized gains insight into the need for cultural contextualization of worship. Church members in non-Western countries do not always appreciate the values in their own cultures as they relate to worship. They are in an ambivalent situation in which they react negatively against their own culture liturgically, while defending and praising and encouraging it historically and socially. Yet, on the other hand, they are vociferous in their insistence that not everything from the West is good. What is good and proper is not always determined on the right basis, by asking: Does it represent what we believe theologically? Does it accurately illustrate what we believe liturgically? Does it represent quality music judged from within its own cultural values? Is it in harmony with Adventist principles of worship and music? So often such judgments are made instead on the basis of association. For example, delightful indigenous instruments are often rejected as inappropriate for use in worship services because they are used locally in non-worship situations. Instead the Western piano and/or organ are preferred, as they are associated with American (and therefore Christian) culture. This preference remains in spite of the fact that both piano and organ are popular in contemporary American rock music. The same is true of hymnals and song books, which contain some Western hymns and songs that are glaringly out of place in many cultural contexts, but which are adopted there anyway.

Why must we be torn between extremes? Why do we so often adopt an either/or instead of a both/and attitude? Why does an acceptance of cultural revivalism have to mean a rejection of the aesthetic? Or the opposite? Why is it we find it so hard, if not impossible, to appreciate and assimilate the good in both? Why do we find it so hard, if not impossible, to appreciate and assimilate liturgically the best in cultural traditions? I do not believe that revelation includes the concretization of the cultural conditions which prevailed during the prophetic and apostolic periods or any other period of world and church history. The truth always remains the same, eternally valid and unchanging, while the cultural setting in which truth is first revealed, through which it is communicated, and in which it is subsequently re-revealed and reaffirmed is relative and changing.

In many non-Christian cultures there exists a well-established, perhaps intuitive understanding of the relationship between idea (concept, truth, doctrine), and the reenactment of that idea artistically (painting, sculpture, music). Human origins, the meaning of life, the crises of life or rites of passage, and important personal, tribal, or national historic events are explained by such reenactments or rituals. Man is by nature a religious being. God made him that way. He was also created an artistic and creative being. He has an inbred need to portray his understanding about life and religion in action, story, and ritual. Even his confrontation with the mysterious, with what he does not and cannot know or adequately explain, he attempts to express dramatically. Just as man is a born religionist, he is also a born ritualist. The need to depict is a natural human trait and has its origins in God the Father, who created the universe and made man in His image. This need must be informed and guided, but it should never be ignored. To say ritual has no place in life or in religion is to misunderstand the nature of man.

We do not believe that man is totally depraved and that consequently he has no higher aspirations, that whatever he produces must automatically be suspect. We believe that even fallen man has retained the image of God, though it is distorted and marred. That image expresses itself in man's highest achievements in drama, music, the graphic arts, and in science and technology. These are, then, points of contact between God and the creatures He has made. This means that even in the most primitive cultures, in non-Christian cultures, there are to be found evidences of the divine image in various forms of artistic expression.

If non-Christian myth can be culturally dramatized and depicted in ceremonial ritual, why cannot Christian truth be illustrated liturgically? Verbal communication is not the only way to pass on truth. In many non-Christian cultures, rites reinforce the beliefs or superstitions of the people. Rites relate the abstract to human feelings and human emotions. They are social acts which make beliefs understood by re-enacting or depicting them in human action, language, and creativity in the arts.

Art in any culture, religious or otherwise, synthesizes perception. It helps put together in the mind what the senses have imaged; it explains how the parts of the whole of life have been put together. Native art is usually representational, descriptive, and realistic rather than abstract, even though it might appear distorted according to certain standards. Much of Western art is understood only by artists, whereas primitive art is meant to be understood by everyone. It is an attempt to find meaning in that which exists or occurs rather than to create an existence of its own. With that attempt conservative Christianity ought to feel comfortable. Ritual performs the same function, though in a different way. It helps to image the myth or truth, whatever the case may be. One of the primary purposes of primitive art is to enhance religious ceremony. That purpose is reflective of the image of God in man even though he may not be Christian man.

Human beings appear to possess the need and the desire to express themselves artistically. If they live where there are an abundance of trees, they will carve. If their environment is the desert, they will develop beautifully intricate sand paintings. Man will find some means of creating that which depicts his search for the meaning of his origins, his life, and his history. In Western countries the artist is a trained professional. In primitive societies artistic talents are more widely distributed among populations. Professional artists are rare. Art is not a profession so much as a vital part of the way of life. A carpenter building a house, if he feels like it, will think nothing of decorating it with elaborate carvings he designs and executes himself. A primary reason for this is community self-sufficiency. Skills are simply there because they are needed and appreciated, and are handed on from one generation to the next.

Primitive peoples think poetically rather than scientifically. Therefore, art becomes part of the thought processes. If we do not understand what they are saying with their art it is not because they are saying nothing. It is because we are viewing what they have created from within an alien Western cultural context and applying the wrong criteria. The same problem is present with ritual. We find it difficult, if not impossible, to accept certain cultural rites because we interpret them with an alien set of values. We are unable to recognize ways in which some cultural rites could be adopted and adapted by the church because we view them from the point of view of a cultural bias rather than on the basis of truth alone.

To visualize in practical terms what has been said above, consider a recent missionary experiment in Thailand. Missionaries there observed that Thai people were reluctant to enter a Western-style church building. They were very interested in what took place inside the building, however, and would crowd the outside to look in the windows and sit nearby so as to hear if they could not see. It was discovered that there were cultural aversions to being trapped inside the heavy and formidable stone or brick walls of a building in the Gothic style so admired in the Western world. In America a Gothic-style church is a *real* church, but to the Thais such a building was threatening. Consequently, when a new church was built, Thai feelings were incorporated architecturally. The church is built of wood, with a low, sloping roof covering a wide veranda all around on which people can gather. It is an elevated type of structure with few walls, giving the impression of openness. No pews or chairs are used; instead the floor is covered with reed mats. The worship center is a small, slightly raised platform covered with the same kind of mats. The missionary pastor does not wait in a "minister's room" until the service begins. Instead he arrives early, seats himself cross-legged in the Thai fashion near the edge of the platform, and chats with the gathering congregation. People drift in leisurely and arrange themselves on the mats while daily events and family affairs are discussed with the pastor. Children mill about freely. At an appropriate time the group organizes itself, parents signal children, who quietly take their places next to their parents. Quiet descends and the service is ready to begin.

Meanwhile the lay leaders who will share the platform have arranged themselves there. No formal procession of platform personnel takes place. The worship service is conducted from the sitting position and there is no moving about by worship leaders. The prayers, the reading of Scripture, the preaching of the sermon, are all done while sitting. The Thai congregation feels more comfortable that way than if the pastor stands and towers over them as he speaks. The general feeling experienced is one of sharing and participating on an informal level, even though all is done very formally. Oriental formality takes place in Thailand in a very informal way.

What has been described above is contextualization of the faith. The people are not threatened by an alien architecture, art, or ritual, and are free, therefore, to deal with the message on its own merits. Thai cultural rituals, especially in connection with weddings, have been retained and given Christian interpretation and meaning. Thai cultural rituals now illustrate and proclaim Christian truths and ideas.

When the Advent message comes wrapped in an indigenous cultural package it does not seem so strange, so foreign, and it is much more readily acceptable. The people are freed to deal with the religious ideas without the confusion of alien cultural trappings. All people have a cultural bias. We must learn to use that bias in a liturgically constructive way, rather than fight against it.

In conclusion one more thing should be said concerning the influence of culture, in this case a negative influence on ritual. It illustrates how a forward-looking church can glorify the past to the point where it is a hindrance to contemporary communication.

Many years ago, during the Lutheran phase of my ministerial life, I was required to take a course entitled "Liturgical Speech." The course was designed to teach potential pastors and worship leaders how to conduct worship services and other occasional services such as weddings and funerals. The main purpose of the course, I began to suspect as the days rolled by, was to teach the class members how to read and speak King James English, and how to pray in that "holy" language of Shakespeare and Queen Elizabeth I!

I was mystified and somewhat disturbed by the fact that although the *Revised Standard Version* of the Bible had just recently appeared (in my judgment one of the best things that has happened to English Christianity in this century), the course was taught as though nothing of such monumental import had occurred. The Scripture lessons and the liturgical prayers found in the *Service Book and Hymnal* of the Lutheran Church still clung to the archaic language of a bygone day. At one point in the worship service I had to wrap my tongue around the phrase, "Wherefore we flee for refuge to thine infinite mercy." Why couldn't I say, "We come to hide in your mercy that never ends"? If I and my congregation spoke every day like the people of King James' and Shakespeare's time, such language would have been most appropriate. But we don't address one another by "thee" and "thou" today. Nor do we say "shouldst," "wouldst," or "believeth."

Eventually the Lutheran Churches published an occasional service book using the modern forms of speech and many pastors and worship leaders heaved grateful sighs of relief. Imagine my consternation when I joined the Seventh-day Adventist Church and heard, during the worship services, determined laymen and ministers struggling with, and horribly mangling, the archaic language of King James! Can you imagine a man who works in a factory all week long, speaking the most crude and common forms of English (like that of the *koine* Greek of the New Testament), trying to bend his tongue around a "shouldst" and a "wouldst" on Sabbath morning? The results would often be laughable if they were not so pathetic and unnecessary.

It would seem we are faced with two alternatives. Either we begin teaching courses in liturgical speech to future ministers and lay leaders, or we start using the language of our own time. We need to be less concerned about antiquity and more concerned about contemporary communication. Perhaps this is why prayer, any prayer, is so difficult for untrained laymen. We have taught them by cultural tradition that prayer is reserved for those who can speak the "holy" language of the seventeenth century. It is strange that this liturgical style is maintained in the so-called "free churches," where prayer should be spontaneous and unencumbered by old cultural forms. I still recall with delight the stumbling prayer of a lay elder who in deep reverence prayed: "Oh our mostedst, holiedst, and graciousedst heavenly Father." That's as far as he got in his prayer, and for the next five minutes I was lost in the struggle to control the rampaging chuckle bubbling within me. If we are going to insist that our faithful and earnest lay brethren participate in worship services as leaders, then perhaps we ought to do them a favor and write out a prayer in old English so they can practice it for a week. But that would be foreign to the "free church" tradition. Perhaps we would be further ahead if we encouraged them to pray as they speak. I think God could stand that much better. I know I could.

A new people with a new life and a new hope singing a new song, ought to sing it in a new language.

Discussion Questions

1. The fact that man was created a ritualistic being has both positive and negative implications for worship. What are they?
2. Does SDA subculture have both positive and negative implications for worship? If so, what are they?
3. How can we learn to become more appreciative of positive cultural values so as to better contextualize both the SDA message and worship in so many lands?

Adventist Worship and Its Meaning / *Part Five*

Worship and Human Response / 14

It was my intention to conclude this book with the previous chapter. After reading the manuscript over a number of times I was fairly well satisfied with the way it had turned out. But the more I read it the more I felt the book was unfinished. Something more was waiting to be said. It could be compared to the last brush stroke on an artist's painting. Without that last brush stroke the painter remains uneasy and the work remains unfinished. After the brush stroke is applied, assuming it is the right one, he knows the job is done. Once it is done another addition would spoil the whole thing. What I say now will be the last thing and I will resist the temptation, that ever plagues the preacher, to keep on talking when I should say "Amen" and sit down.

What needs to be said in conclusion, it seems to me, is something having to do with human response in worship. I have the feeling it could best be said in personal terms. All through the text which you have just read I have tried to weave the warp of theological insight and the woof of personal conviction and story. I will do the same in these concluding remarks, but with the greater emphasis on the personal.

I want to say something first about the Christian who has crossed the threshold from ignorance of God to the worship of God. How can he/she be characterized? He has died with Christ yet still lives in this present age. He has risen with Christ, yet day by day he approaches his physical death. Work provides him with the opportunity to exercise and utilize his creativity and strength, while at the same time his work makes him aware of human limitations. In his worship he avails himself of divine power and strength, yet he always does so as a needy and dependent creature, a supplicant. He is a new creature in Christ, born of water and the Spirit, yet in the flesh he is not free of his old nature. He is in the Spirit yet exposed to all the temptations of the flesh. He is covered with the righteousness of Christ imputed to him, yet still a sinner before God. When he comes into God's presence he cannot come in self-righteousness; he must come in the imputed righteousness of Christ or he cannot come at all. He is *simil justus et peccator*, both justified saint and sinner. He is involved in the reality of life in this world, in the flesh, and in the new life in Christ, in the Spirit. He is that because he is human, not divine, and is *in via*. He is an interim creature. He is a creature of two worlds and is intensely conscious of that fact. His life is one of uneasiness, therefore, because the two realms of his existence are in conflict and will be until Jesus comes. His energies are spent in service to God and thus in service to the world, yet while he so engages himself he continually casts longing eyes heavenward.

Because he is this kind of creature and lives this kind of ambivalent life, this Christian needs to worship with God's people, who share in both corporality and corporateness as Christ's body, the church. Worshiping with others who face the same dilemmas helps the Christian meet and handle the basic ambivalence of the converted life. Corporate worship reflects this ambivalence, this interim between the new birth and the new earth. It takes place between baptism and glory. While this worship on earth is a foretaste of worship in heavenly splendor, it is worship conscious of the world and its need for redemption and hope. The worshiping church is the "called out," while at the same time it is the "sent out." What happens in worship, therefore, will be a repetitive reenactment, a retelling of the story of that calling out and sending in terms of the worshiper's own personal story. Worship offers salvation and service anew in the preached Word and the sacramental Word.

I am the Christian described above. My physical life began in 1929, while my Christian life began in 1952. Instead of fifty-three, I am really only thirty years old! For the past thirty years I have been a worshiper of God and a churchgoer. I have tried to be consistent and regular in worship attendance. In those thirty years of new life I have never deliberately missed the weekly worship of the church except for illness and unavoidable circumstances. Why, I now ask myself? What is there about the gathered church that attracts me week after week, that draws me like an irresistible magnetic force? Has it become nothing more than a habit with no real meaning? At this point in my life perhaps a reassessment would be helpful. Why is it that in spite of the inanity heard so often from the pulpit, in spite of the ritual ambiguity, in spite of the often tedious inclusion of irrelevancies, in spite of the crudity and unpreparedness of so many worship leaders, in spite of the offense to my aesthetic senses, I continue to attend?

Why do I participate in all of the strange activities of the church, which seem so foreign and sometimes out of place in the real world of modern times? No matter how hard I try, the soaring melodies of organ and united voices do not drown out the strident cries of the world around me. The walls of the beautiful sanctuary in which I worship never successfully hide from my view the truth concerning the people, the neighborhood, the world, which surround it. While I listen attentively and even eagerly to the sermon which describes in glowing terms the glories of heaven and the soon-coming Saviour, my mind refuses to be wooed completely away from the very real concerns and problems of life in the world. And if, for some mysterious reason, my worship experience does transport me to unseen realms and fill my being with peace and joy, I cannot remain for long in the sanctuary. I must leave again that blessed place and enter the real world where my life must be lived, where I am to be Christian. I would like to stay in the sanctuary because that would be the easiest. But my Lord, having fortified me with His spiritual treasure, sends me out to be church even though that is the hardest.

For the Christian the one experience seems to demand the other. My life in the world, with its tensions and uncertainties, its demands and challenges, sends me weekly to the sanctuary, where I draw strength from the divine Source and from the gathered Body of Christ. My experience there, during which I hear again of His love for me and see it reenacted in the liturgy of baptism, footwashing, and Holy Communion, in which I hear and see His love for a fallen and sad world in the same way, sends me back again into that world.

The church is the only place where the really basic questions about life are asked and answered. They may not always be asked astutely, but they are asked. They may not always be answered profoundly or well, but a good attempt is made and that I appreciate. The minister who faithfully and honestly tries to the best of his ability deserves my gratitude.

The questions I ask are natural to the human soul. Everyone asks them in some form or other. I'm so glad to have found the place where they are asked openly and without fear or hesitation. My questions are not considered morbid or depressing or irrelevant, because the church exists to help me with the answers. Where did I come from? Why am I alive? Where am I going? What am I supposed to do? My questions have to do with the origin, the purpose, the meaning, and the disposition of my life. I cannot rule the world, move nations, solve international problems, curb inflation, conquer the universe, run for president. Such things are mind-boggling in scope and present challenges that seem insurmountable. I can hardly manage my own personal affairs, to say nothing of what Paul calls the body of sin which dwells within me. Yet I still ask questions about why I am here and where I am going, and I need answers that help me meet the challenges I face each day.

My need for answers to center-core questions produces the need for church, for worship. So I go back again and again. My hunger for the God-dimension must be satisfied. Living, as I do, in the midst of the fear and hate that are in this world, I need the Word of power, of transformation, of hope. I need to face the questions concerning the reason my world is in the mess it's in. I go to church because I find it impossible to stop asking such questions, because my need to know is acute, because I have sensed that the church's answers make the most sense. What I hear when I worship makes me nod my head in agreement and add my voice to the chorus of "Amens." They are the same old words I have heard so many times during the past thirty years, but they are always new. They are not worn-out clichés to me. They are life and breath. They speak to me on a level no other speech could reach.

Most of all I go to worship because there I meet my Lord, and there I meet His people. It comforts me to know that there are a lot of other people just like me, asking the same questions. I go to church because it helps me find my place in history. My personal history is part of that history which goes back through the sixteenth century to the time of the apostles, back to creation itself, and that also continues forward into the unknown future that is anticipated in God's Word. Having caught this vision of God's plans for me, I must respond. The Bible calls such response "glorying" and "praising" and "remembering" and "worshiping." It finds its most satisfying expression in the *sanctus:* "Holy, holy, holy, is the Lord of hosts, the whole earth is full of His glory."

I leave the sanctuary only to discover that I am still in the same old world. But I am not the same old man. I have had a transfusion of spiritual nourishment that provides power and life. I can face life anew, reformed, refreshed, refilled, revived, and return once again to my tasks and responsibilities while waiting for the return of my Lord. I am a new man in Christ and I sing a new song!

MARANATHA!

Appendices

Suggested Orders of Service / A

If those who worship in Seventh-day Adventist churches are to be refined, ennobled, and sanctified by means of their worship, then the content of that worship must make possible such results. The planning of worship services cannot be left to whim and fancy, for "the house of God on earth is the gate of heaven. The song of praise, the prayer, the words spoken by Christ's representative, are God's appointed agencies to prepare a people for the Church above, for that loftier worship into which there can enter nothing that defileth."[1] This is the enunciation of a high and exalted principle for worship among Seventh-day Adventists. It means, in practice, that only the best quality of order, music, preaching, and teaching that the church can produce should be included. Reverence, dignity, and solemnity are essential to the atmosphere of such exalted worship, leading to a sense of holy awe in the presence of God. Elevated views and ideas are called for in the planning and ordering of Adventist worship, especially as the remnant church draws closer in time to the heavenly worship so graphically described in Revelation 4–5. Something of that worship in heavenly splendor should be experienced by every Seventh-day Adventist congregation on every Sabbath.

There are two basic theological foci in Ellen G. White's concept of worship. The first is the transcendence and sovereignty of God, as described in *Testimonies*, Vol. 5, pp. 491–505. Recognition of God's transcendence results in a certain kind of behavior in the house of God—behavior characterized by sacredness, solemnity, dignity, quietness, and a spirit of devotion. The emphasis is on the formal aspects of

[1]White, *Testimonies for the Church*, Vol. 5, p. 491. See Appendix B.

worship. The second focus in Ellen White's concept of worship is the immanence of God, expressed in *Steps to Christ*, pp. 101–104. Awareness of God's immanence encourages worship behavior characterized by fellowship with Him and other believers, mutual encouragement, naturalness, cheerfulness, and a deep consciousness of God's love and care. The emphasis is on the informal aspects of worship.

The planning of SDA worship ought to keep these two foci in balance and provide room for both.

Practically speaking, therefore, the first part of the order of service should be more formal in nature. The sacredness of the sanctuary and of the service itself should be made evident by an attitude of solemnity and devotion on the part of worshipers and worship leaders. Nothing extraneous should be allowed to disrupt the congregation's acknowledgement of the transcendent God, who is holy, almighty, and the righteous Lover and Judge of mankind. Announcements and church business should not intrude upon the service and should be confined to a period prior to the worship leaders' taking their places and the beginning of worship proper. The call to worship, the invocation, the introit, and the opening hymn should provide the formal, transcendent emphasis.

The Scripture reading, the prayer, the sermon, and the special music are elements that move the worshiping congregation to an awareness of the immanence of God, of His presence by His Spirit among His people to bless them through Word and sacrament. Here the emphasis shifts from the congregation's address to God, to God's address to the congregation, followed by or intermingled with their joyful response in song, praise, gratitude, sacrificial giving, and the receiving of His gifts offered in Word and sacrament. Thus the informal aspects of worship are also present.

Following are four suggested orders of service. Numbers 1 and 2 are more elaborate and formal in nature, and numbers 3 and 4 are less formal and more abbreviated.

Service 1

THE ORDER OF WORSHIP

(Name of Church)

(Date)

Sabbath Worship Begins

** The Prelude
The Call to Worship
* The Introit
The Invocation
The Opening Hymn #000

Christ Speaks From Heaven

** The Written Word:
† The Pastoral Prayer
The Prayer Response
** The Offering
* The Doxology
** The Special Music/or Hymn
The Preached Word:

Worship Ends—Service Begins

* The Closing Hymn #000
The Benediction
The Benedictory Response
** The Postlude

** Congregation seated * Congregation stands † Congregation kneels

(*NOTE:* The action indicated by the asterisks and cross continues until a subsequent mark appears.)

The words and music for the introit, prayer response, and benedictory response follow the suggestions on pages 171–173.

Service 1 represents a traditional type of service within the Adventist practice in that the offering and prayer precede the sermon. For an explanation of the designation "Christ Speaks From Heaven," see my book *It's a Two-Way Street*, chapters 7–8.

The introit, prayer response, and benedictory response chosen should provide the liturgical illustration of the ecumenical doctrines of the Seventh-day Adventist Church, given by the Lord, as we believe, to call His church into the unity He desires just prior to His return.

Service 2

THE SERVICE OF CELEBRATION

(Name of Church)

(Date)

The Celebration of the Word

** With Prelude
With the Call to Worship
* With Invocation
With Introit
With Hearing the Written Word:
With Singing Hymn #000
** With Hearing the Preached Word:

The Celebration of Praise

† With Prayer
With Prayer Response
** With Sacrifice in Giving
* With the Doxology
** With Special Music/or Anthem
With Testimony
* With Singing Hymn #000
With Benediction
With Benedictory Response
** With Postlude

** Congregation seated   * Congregation stands   † Congregation kneels

(NOTE: The action indicated by the asterisks and cross continues until a subsequent mark appears.)

Words and music for the introit, prayer response, and benedictory response are the same as for Service 1.

This order represents a change from the traditional sequence in that the sermon precedes the prayer and the offering, which are seen to be responses of the congregation to the Word of God in Scripture and sermon.

The emphasis in this service, in harmony with Adventist thought, is on the centrality of the Word of God in its written and spoken forms, to which the believing congregation responds in grateful praise. God speaks first, then the worshipers answer appropriately.

In harmony with the counsel of Ellen G. White, a testimony by a selected member of the congregation, or a visitor, is included.

For this service the platform personnel may enter as the organist plays "Break Thou the Bread of Life," which signals the congregation to rise. The first elder may carry the preaching Bible reverently to the pulpit and then take his place kneeling in unison with the worship leaders. This liturgical action dramatically calls attention to the centrality of the Word in the worship service.

When occasional services are a part of the order of service the following may be included as the second part of Service 2:

The Celebration of Praise in Communion

With Footwashing
** With Singing Hymn #000
With the Lord's Supper[1]
With Sacrifice in Giving[2]
* With Doxology
** With Testimony
* With Singing Hymn #000
With Benediction
With Benedictory Response
** With Postlude

[1]The distribution follows the reading of appropriate Scripture and prayers of consecration. It is important to remember that it is the congregation that needs consecration so that it may corporately be conscious of the need to be broken bread and poured-out wine for the sake of the world.

[2]The offering at this point becomes a response to God's gifts in Word and sacrament, symbolizing liturgically the giving of oneself to Him who gives all.

The Celebration of Praise in Baptism

† With Prayer[1]
** With Examination of Candidates
With Testimony of Candidates
With Special Music/or Anthem[2]
With Baptism
With Sacrifice in Giving[3]
* With Doxology
With Benediction
With Benedictory Response
** With Postlude

[1]The candidates should be included in this general prayer.

[2]At this point the candidates will prepare for baptism. If additional time is

needed a song service can be conducted.

[3]The offering at this point becomes a response to God's gifts in Word and sacrament.

The Celebration of Praise in Dedication

† With Prayer[1]
** With Singing Hymn #000[2]
With the Presentation[3]
With the Prayer of Dedication[4]
With the Exhortation[5]
With Sacrifice in Giving[6]
* With Doxology
With Benediction
With Benedictory Response
** With Postlude

[1]The children to be dedicated should be included in this general prayer.

[2]This hymn should be appropriate to the occasion of dedication.

[3]The parents present their child(ren) before God, the Father, by placing him/her in the minister's arms, liturgically symbolizing the giving of the child(ren) to God.

[4]Taking the hand of the mother, liturgically symbolizing family unity, the father prays the dedicatory prayer. After this the minister returns the child to the mother's arms, liturgically symbolizing the parents' responsibility to train the child in the nurture and admonition of the Lord.

[5]The minister exhorts the congregation as to its responsibility, as the family of God, for the child(ren)'s growth as a member of a Christian community. He may say appropriate words with respect to the importance of Christian education and schools.

[6]The offering at this point becomes a response to the gifts of God in Word and in the tender life (lives) now received and dedicated.

Service 3

THE WORSHIP CELEBRATION OF THE
(NAME)
SEVENTH-DAY ADVENTIST
CHURCH

(Date)

The Celebration of the Word

** With Prelude
* With Introit
With Invocation
With the Written Word:
With Hymn #000
** With the Spoken Word:

The Celebration of Praise

† With Prayer
** With Special Music/or Anthem
With Offering
* With Doxology
** With Testimony
* With Hymn #000
With Benediction
** With Postlude

** Congregation seated ** Congregation stands *† Congregation kneels

(*NOTE:* The action indicated by the asterisks and cross continues until a subsequent mark appears.)

This is an abbreviated version of Service 2 in which the prayer and benedictory response are omitted. It remains the same with respect to sequence in that the emphasis is on the centrality of the Word of God, to which the congregation responds.

As in Service 2, this service includes a testimony.

The introit may be selected by the worship committee, an example being the first verse of "Blessed Jesus, at Thy Word . . .".

In this service as in Service 2, the preacher may also lead in the prayer that follows the sermon, during which the congregation kneels. When the prayer follows the sermon the substance of the prayer can be more relevantly related to God's speech in the sermon; thus preaching and praying become dialogical.

Service 4

THE ORDER OF SERVICE

Praising

Song Leader: Tom Jones
Hymns
111
222
333
444
Special Music /or Anthem

Preaching

"Sermon Title"
Text
Preacher: John Johnson

Praying

Theme Hymn #000
Prayer in Groups
Benediction: Harry Harrison

This service is intended to be very informal in nature. Beginning with a song service that sets the tone for the hearing of the spoken Word, it moves through proclamation to response in prayer.

This service provides much participation on the part of the worshipers, maintains the centrality of the Word, and provides for prayer as the response to the Word, making the service dialogical in nature.

This service would be most appropriate for vespers, for youth meetings, for camp meetings and retreats.

An offering is not included, although it could easily be done as an element of prayer, symbolizing the giving of oneself to the God who has spoken through the Word.

Suggested responses:

The Introit

With joy we hail the sacred day
Which God has called His own;
With joy the summons we obey,
To worship at His throne.

Then hail! thou sacred, blessed day.
The best of all the seven.
When hearts unite their vows to pay
Of gratitude to heaven.

The Prayer Response

Where high the heavenly temple stands,
The house of God not made with hands,
A great High Priest our nature wears,
The guardian of mankind, He hears.

The Benedictory Response

We have this hope that burns within our hearts,
Hope in the coming of the Lord.
We have this faith that Christ alone imparts,
Faith in the promise of His Word.
We believe the time is here
When the nations far and near
Shall awake, and shout, and sing—
Hallelujah! Christ is King!
We have this hope that burns within our hearts,
Hope in the coming of the Lord.

With Joy We Hail the Sacred Day

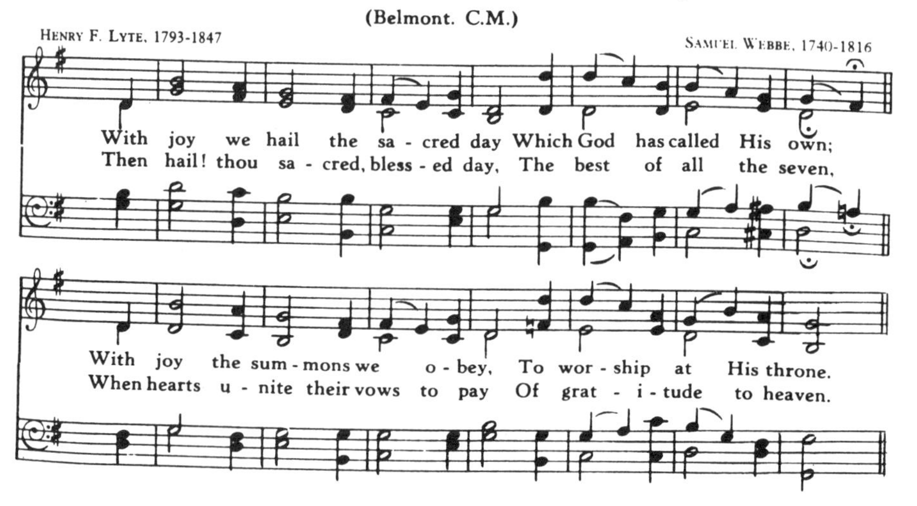

Where High the Heavenly Temple Stands

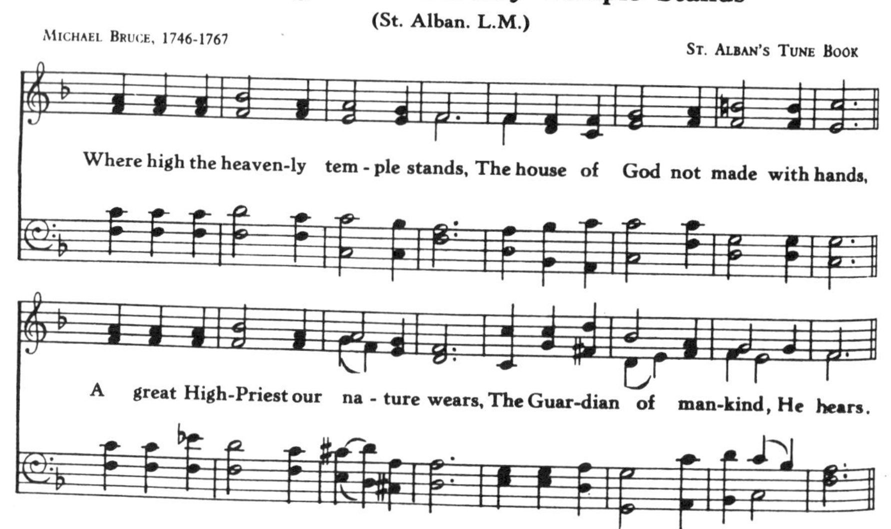

We Have This Hope

Selected Comments on Worship by Ellen G. White / B

Our meetings should be made intensely interesting. They should be pervaded with the very atmosphere of heaven. Let there by no long, dry speeches and formal prayers merely for the sake of occupying the time. All should be ready to act their part with promptness, and when their duty is done, the meeting should be closed. Thus the interest will be kept up to the last. This is offering to God acceptable worship. His service should be made interesting and attractive and not be allowed to degenerate into a dry form. We must live for Christ minute by minute, hour by hour, and day by day; then Christ will dwell in us, and when we meet together, His love will be in our hearts, welling up like a spring in the desert, refreshing all, and making those who are ready to perish, eager to drink of the waters of life.

Testimonies for the Church, Vol. 5, p. 609

Is it not your duty to put some skill and study and planning into the matter of conducting religious meetings—how they shall be conducted so as to do the greatest amount of good, and leave the very best impression upon all who attend? You plan in regard to your temporal labors. If you learn a trade, you seek to improve year by year in experience, executing plans that shall show progression in your work. Is your temporal business of as much consequence as the service of God? matters where eternal interests are involved? God is displeased with your lifeless manner in His house, your sleepy indifferent ways of conducting religious worship. You need to bear in mind that you attend divine service to meet with God, to be refreshed, comforted, blessed, not to do a duty imposed upon you.

Review and Herald, April 14, 1885

God is high and holy; and to the humble, believing soul, His house on earth, the place where His people meet for worship, is as the gate of heaven. The song of praise, the words spoken by Christ's ministers, are God's appointed agencies to prepare a people for the church above, for that loftier worship.

My Life Today, p. 186

Through the psalmist God declares, "Whoso offereth praise glorifieth me." Much of the public worship of God consists of praise and prayer, and every follower of Christ should engage in this worship. There is also the preaching service conducted by those whose work it is to instruct the congregation in the Word of God. Although all are not called to minister in word and doctrine, they need not be cold and responseless listeners. When the Word of God was spoken to the Hebrews anciently, the Lord said to Moses, "And let all the people say, Amen." This response, in the fervor of their souls, was required as evidence that they understood the word spoken and were interested in it.

Signs of the Times, June 24, 1886

A mere form of Christianity is not of the least value. It is destitute of saving power, having in it no reformative energy. A religion which is confined to Sabbath worship emits no rays of light to others.

Testimonies for the Church, Vol. 5, p. 339

By the first angel, men are called upon to "fear God, and give glory to Him" and to worship Him as the Creator of the heavens and the earth. In order to do this, they must obey His law. . . . Without obedience to His commandments no worship can be pleasing to God.

The duty to worship God is based upon the fact that He is the Creator and that to Him all other beings owe their existence. And wherever, in the Bible, His claim to reverence and worship, above the gods of the heathen, is presented, there is cited the evidence of His creative power.

"The importance of the Sabbath as the memorial of creation is that it keeps ever present the true reason why worship is due to God"—because He is the Creator, and we are His creatures. "The Sabbath therefore lies at the very foundation of divine worship, for it teaches this great truth in the most impressive manner, and no other institution does this. The true ground of divine worship, not of that on the seventh day merely, but of all worship, is found in the distinction between the Creator and His creatures. This great fact can never become obsolete, and must never be forgotten." J. N. Andrews, *History of the Sabbath,* chapter 27. It was to keep this truth ever before the minds of men, that God instituted the Sabbath in Eden; and so long as the fact that He is our Creator continues to be a reason why we should worship Him, so long the Sabbath will continue as its sign and memorial.

Great Controversy, pp. 437, 438

Although God dwells not in temples made with hands, yet He honors with His presence the assemblies of His people. He has promised that when they come together to seek Him, to acknowledge their sins, and to pray for one another, He will meet with them by His Spirit. But those who assemble to worship Him should put away every evil thing. Unless they worship Him in spirit and truth and in the beauty of holiness, their coming together will be of no avail.

Prophets and Kings, p. 50

Brethren, unless you educate yourselves to respect the place of devotion, you will receive no blessing from God. You may worship Him in form, but there will be no spiritual service. "Where two or three are gathered together in My name," says Jesus, "there am I in the midst of them." All should feel that they are in the divine presence, and instead of dwelling upon the faults and errors of others they should be diligently searching their own hearts.

Testimonies for the Church, Vol. 5, p. 608

Nothing that is sacred, nothing that pertains to the worship of God, should be treated with carelessness and indifference. When the word of life is spoken, you should remember that you are listening to the voice of God through His delegated servant.

Messages to Young People, p. 266

Many want to do things after their own style; they object to consultation, and are impatient under leadership. Well-matured plans are needed in the service of God. Common sense is an excellent thing in the worship of the Lord. The thinking powers should be consecrated to Christ, and ways and means should be devised to serve Him best.

Testimonies for the Church, Vol. 4, pp. 70, 71

A congregation may be the poorest in the land. It may be without the attractions of outward show; but if the members possess the principles of the character of Christ, angels will unite with them in their worship.

Prophets and Kings, pp. 565, 566

Those who receive the light of truth are to have lesson upon lesson to educate them not to keep silent, but to speak often one to another. They are to keep in mind the Sabbath meeting, when those who love and fear God, and who think upon His name, can have opportunity to express their thoughts in speaking one to another. . . .

Let each one seek to become an intelligent Christian, bearing his responsibility, and acting his personal part to make the meeting interesting and profitable.

Seventh-day Adventist Bible Commentary, Vol. 4, p. 1183

It is the will of God that those who engage in His work shall be subject to one another. His worship must be conducted with consistency, unity and sound judgment.

Testimonies for the Church, Vol. 5, p. 270

In their efforts to reach the people, the Lord's messengers are not to follow the ways of the world. In the meetings that are held, they are not to depend on worldly singers and theatrical display to awaken an interest. . . . How can the heavenly choir join in music that is only a form?

The evil of formal worship cannot be too strongly depicted, but no words can properly set forth the deep blessedness of genuine worship. When human beings sing with the spirit and the understanding, heavenly musicians take up the strain and join in the song of thanksgiving.

Testimonies for the Church, Vol. 9, p. 143

The most eloquent prayers are but idle words if they do not express the true sentiments of the heart. But the prayer that comes from an earnest heart, when the simple wants of the soul are expressed as we would ask an earthly friend for a favor, expecting it to be granted—this is the prayer of faith. God does not desire our ceremonial compliments; but the unspoken cry of the heart broken and subdued with a sense of its sin and utter weakness, finds its way to the Father of all mercy.

Thoughts from the Mount of Blessing, pp. 129, 130

Those who are most superficial generally have the most to say. Their prayers are long and mechanical. They weary the angels and the people who listen to them. Our prayers should be short and right to the point. Let the long, tiresome petitions be left for the closet, if any have such to offer. Let the Spirit of God into your hearts, and it will sweep away all dry formality.

Testimonies for the Church, Vol. 4, p. 70

Religion is not to be confined to external forms and ceremonies. The religion that comes from God is the only religion that will lead to God. In order to serve Him aright, we must be born of the divine Spirit. This will purify the heart and renew the mind, giving us a new capacity for knowing and loving God. It will give us a willing obedience to all His requirements. This is true worship. It is the fruit of the working of the Holy Spirit.

Desire of Ages, p. 189

At the same time the Jews were, by their sins, separating themselves from God. They were unable to discern the deep spiritual significance of their symbolic service. In their self-righteousness they trusted to their own works, to the sacrifices and ordinances themselves, instead of relying upon the merits of Him to whom all these things pointed. Thus "going about to establish their own righteousness" (Romans 10:3), they built themselves up in a self-sufficient formalism. Wanting the Spirit and grace of God, they tried to make up for the lack by a rigorous observance of religious ceremonies and rites. Not content with the ordinances which God Himself had appointed, they encumbered the divine commands with countless exactions of their own devising. The greater their distance from God, the more rigorous they were in the observance of these forms.

Prophets and Kings, pp. 708, 709

Everything about the priests and rulers—their dress, customs, ceremonies, traditions—made them unfit to be the light of the world. They looked upon themselves, the Jewish nation, as the world. But Christ commissioned His disciples to proclaim a faith and worship that would have in it nothing of caste or country, a faith that would be adapted to all peoples, all nations, all classes of men.

Desire of Ages, p. 820

It is when the vital principles of the kingdom of God are lost sight of, that ceremonies become multitudinous and extravagant. It is when the character building is neglected, when the adornment of the soul is lacking, when the simplicity of godliness is despised, that pride and love of display demand magnificent church edifices, splendid adornings, and imposing ceremonials. But in all this God is not honored. He values His church, not for its external advantages, but for the sincere piety which distinguishes it from the world. He estimates it according to the growth of its members in the knowledge of Christ, according to their progress in spiritual experience.

Prophets and Kings, p. 565

Christ saw that something must be done. Numerous ceremonies were enjoined upon the people without the proper instruction as to their import. The worshipers offered their sacrifices without understanding that they were typical of the only perfect Sacrifice. And among them, unrecognized and unhonored, stood the One symbolized by all their service. He had given directions in regard to the offerings, He understood their symbolical value, and He saw that they were now perverted and misunderstood. Spiritual worship was fast disappearing. No link bound the priests and rulers to their God. Christ's work was to establish an altogether different worship.

Desire of Ages, p. 157

Its gorgeous display and solemn rites fascinate the senses of the people and silence the voice of reason and of conscience. The eye is charmed. Magnificent churches, imposing processions, golden altars, jeweled shrines, choice paintings, exquisite sculpture appeal to the love of beauty. The ear also is captivated. The music is unsurpassed. The rich notes of the deep-toned organ, blending with the melody of many voices as it swells through the lofty domes and pillared aisles of her grand cathedrals, cannot fail to impress the mind with awe and reverence.

This outward splendor, pomp, and ceremony, that only mocks the longings of the sin-sick soul, is an evidence of inward corruption. The religion of Christ needs not such attractions to recommend it. In the light shining from the cross, true Christianity appears so pure and lovely that no external decorations can enhance its true worth. It is the beauty of holiness, a meek and quiet spirit, which is of value with God.

Brilliancy of style is not necessarily an index of pure, elevated thought. High conceptions of art, delicate refinement of taste, often exist in minds that are earthly and sensual.

A religion of externals is attractive to the unrenewed heart. . . . Thousands who have not an experimental knowledge of Christ will be led to accept the form of godliness without the power. Such a religion is just what the multitudes desire.

Great Controversy, pp. 566, 567

Mrs. White's most inclusive statement on the subject of corporate worship is found in *Testimonies for the Church,* Vol. 5, pp. 491–500. For your convenience this is appended. For further study see the *Index to the Writings of Ellen G. White* under such headings as "Worship of God," "Church Services," "Public Prayer," "Sabbath Services," "Religious Service," and others.

BEHAVIOR IN THE HOUSE OF GOD

To the humble, believing soul, the house of God on earth is the gate of heaven. The song of praise, the prayer, the words spoken by Christ's representatives, are God's appointed agencies to prepare a people for the church above, for that loftier worship into which there can enter nothing that defileth.

From the sacredness which was attached to the earthly sanctuary, Christians may learn how they should regard the place where the Lord meets with His people. There has been a great change, not for the better, but for the worse, in the habits and customs of the people in reference to religious worship. The precious, the sacred, things which connect us with God are fast losing their hold upon our minds and hearts, and are being brought down to the level of common things. The reverence which the people had anciently for the sanctuary where they met with God in sacred service has largely passed away. Nevertheless, God Himself gave the order of His service, exalting it high above everything of a temporal nature.

The house is the sanctuary for the family, and the closet or the grove the most retired place for individual worship; but the church is the sanctuary for the congregation. There should be rules in regard to the time, the place, and the manner of worshiping. Nothing that is sacred, nothing that pertains to the worship of God, should be treated with carelessness or indifference. In order that men may do their best work in showing forth the praises of God, their associations must be such as will keep the sacred distinct from the common, in their minds. Those who have broad ideas, noble thoughts and aspirations, are those who have associations that strengthen all thoughts of divine things. Happy are those who have a sanctuary, be it high or low, in the city or among the rugged mountain caves, in the lowly cabin or in the wilderness. If it is the best they can secure for the Master, He will hallow the place with His presence, and it will be holy unto the Lord of hosts.

When the worshipers enter the place of meeting, they should do so with decorum, passing quietly to their seats. If there is a stove in the room, it is not proper to crowd about it in an indolent, careless attitude. Common talking, whispering, and laughing should not be permitted in the house of worship, either before or after the service. Ardent, active piety should characterize the worshipers.

If some have to wait a few minutes before the meeting begins, let them maintain a true spirit of devotion by silent meditation, keeping the heart uplifted to God in prayer that the service may be of special benefit to their own hearts and lead to the conviction and conversion of other souls. They should remember that heavenly messengers are in the house. We all lose much sweet communion with God by our restlessness, by not encouraging moments of reflection and prayer. The spiritual condition needs to be often reviewed and the mind and heart drawn toward the Sun of Righteousness. If when the people come into the house of worship, they have genuine reverence for the Lord and bear in mind that they are in His presence, there will be a sweet eloquence in silence. The whispering and laughing and talking which might be without sin in a common business place should find no sanction in the house where God is worshiped. The mind should be prepared to hear the word of God, that it may have due weight and suitably impress the heart.

When the minister enters, it should be with dignified, solemn mien. He should bow down in silent prayer as soon as he steps into the pulpit, and earnestly ask help of God. What an impression this will make! There will be solemnity and awe upon the people. Their minister is communing with God; he is committing himself to God before he dares to stand before the people. Solemnity rests upon all, and angels of God are brought very near. Every one of the congregation, also, who fears God should with bowed head unite in silent prayer with him that God may grace the meeting with His presence and give power to His truth proclaimed from human lips. When the meeting is opened by prayer, every knee should bow in the presence of the Holy One, and every heart should ascend to God in silent devotion. The prayers of faithful worshipers will be heard, and the ministry of the word will prove effectual. The lifeless attitude of the worshipers in the house of God is one great reason why the ministry is not more productive of good. The melody of song, poured forth from many hearts in clear, distinct utterance, is one of God's instrumentalities in the work of saving souls. All the service should be conducted with solemnity and awe, as if in the visible presence of the Master of assemblies.

When the word is spoken, you should remember, brethren, that you are listening to the voice of God through His delegated servant. Listen attentively. Sleep not for one instant, because by this slumber you may lose the very words that you need most—the very words which, if heeded, would save your feet from straying into wrong paths. Satan and his angels are busy creating a paralyzed condition of the senses so that cautions, warnings, and reproofs shall not be heard; or if heard, that they shall not take effect upon the heart and reform the life. Sometimes a little child may so attract the attention of the hearers that the precious seed does not fall into good ground and bring forth fruit. Sometimes young men and women have so little reverence for the house and worship of God that they keep up a continual communication with each other during the sermon. Could these see the angels of God looking upon them and marking their doings, they would be filled with shame, with abhorrence of themselves. God wants attentive hearers. It was while men slept that Satan sowed his tares.

When the benediction is pronounced, all should still be quiet, as if fearful of losing the peace of Christ. Let all pass out without jostling or loud talking, feeling that they are in the presence of God, that His eye is resting upon them, and that they must act as in His visible presence. Let there be no stopping in the aisles to visit or gossip, thus blocking them up so that others cannot pass out.

The precincts of the church should be invested with a sacred reverence. It should not be made a place to meet old friends and visit and introduce common thoughts and worldly business transactions. These should be left outside the church. God and angels have been dishonored by the careless, noisy laughing and shuffling of feet heard in some places.

Parents, elevate the standard of Christianity in the minds of your children; help them to weave Jesus into their experience; teach them to have the highest reverence for the house of God and to understand that when they enter the Lord's house it should be with hearts that are softened and subdued by such thoughts as these: "God is here; this is His house. I must have pure thoughts and the holiest motives. I must have no pride, envy, jealousy, evil surmising, hatred, or deception in my heart, for I am coming into the presence of the holy God. This is the place where God meets with and blesses His people. The high and holy One who inhabiteth eternity looks upon me, searches my heart, and reads the most secret thoughts and acts of my life."

Brethren, will you not devote a little thought to this subject and notice how you conduct yourselves in the house of God and what efforts you are making by precept and example to cultivate reverence in your children? You roll vast responsibilities upon the preacher and hold him accountable for the souls of your children; but you do not sense your own responsibility as parents and as instructors and, like Abraham, command your household after you, that they may keep the statutes of the Lord. Your sons and daughters are corrupted by your own example and lax precepts; and, notwithstanding this lack of domestic training, you expect the minister to counteract your daily work and accomplish the wonderful achievement of training their hearts and lives to virtue and piety. After the minister has done all he can do for the church by faithful, affectionate admonition, patient discipline, and fervent prayer to reclaim and save the soul, yet is not successful, the fathers and mothers often blame him because their children are not converted, when it may be because of their own neglect. The burden rests with the parents; and will they take up the work that God has entrusted to them, and with fidelity perform it? Will they move onward and upward, working in a humble, patient, persevering way to reach the exalted standard themselves and to bring their children up with them? No wonder our churches are feeble and do not have that deep, earnest piety in their borders that they should have. Our present habits and customs, which dishonor God and bring the sacred and heavenly down to the level of the common, are against us. We have a sacred, testing, sanctifying truth; and if our habits and practices are not in accordance with the truth, we are sinners against great light, and are proportionately guilty. It will be far more tolerable for the heathen in the day of God's retributive justice than for us.

A much greater work might be done than we are now doing in reflecting the light of truth. God expects us to bear much fruit. He expects greater zeal and faithfulness, more affectionate and earnest efforts, by the individual members of the church for their neighbors and for those who are out of Christ. Parents must begin their work on a high plane of action. All who name the name of Christ must put on the whole armor and entreat, warn, and seek to win souls from sin.

Lead all you can to listen to the truth in the house of God. We must do much more than we are doing to snatch souls from the burning.

It is too true that reverence for the house of God has become almost extinct. Sacred things and places are not discerned; the holy and exalted are not appreciated. Is there not a cause for the want of fervent piety in our families? Is it not because the high standard of religion is left to trail in the dust? God gave rules of order, perfect and exact, to His ancient people. Has His character changed? Is He not the great and mighty God who rules in the heaven of heavens? Would it not be well for us often to read the directions given by God Himself to the Hebrews, that we who have the light of the glorious truth shining upon us may imitate their reverence for the house of God? We have abundant reason to maintain a fervent, devoted spirit in the worship of God. We have reason even to be more thoughtful and reverential in our worship than had the Jews. But an enemy has been at work to destroy our faith in the sacredness of Christian worship.

The place dedicated to God should not be a room where worldly business is transacted. If the children assemble to worship God in a room that has been used during the week for a school or a storeroom, they will be more than human if, mingled with their devotional thoughts, they do not also have thoughts of their studies or of things that have happened during the week. The education and training of the youth should be of a character that would exalt sacred things and encourage pure devotion for God in His house. Many who profess to be children of the heavenly King have no true appreciation of the sacredness of eternal things. Nearly all need to be taught how to conduct themselves in the house of God. Parents should not only teach, but command, their children to enter the sanctuary with sobriety and reverence.

The moral taste of the worshipers in God's holy sanctuary must be elevated, refined, sanctified. This matter has been sadly neglected. Its importance has been overlooked, and as the result, disorder and irreverence have become prevalent, and God has been dishonored. When the leaders in the church, ministers and people, father and mothers, have not had elevated views of this matter, what could be expected of the inexperienced children? They are too often found in groups, away from the parents, who should have charge of them. Notwithstanding they are in the presence of God, and His eye is looking upon them, they are light and trifling, they whisper and laugh, are careless, irreverent, and inattentive. They are seldom instructed that the minister is God's ambassador, that the message he brings is one of God's appointed agencies in the salvation of souls, and that to all who have the privilege brought within their reach it will be a savor of life unto life or of death unto death.

The delicate and susceptible minds of the youth obtain their estimate of the labors of God's servants by the way their parents treat the matter. Many heads of families make the service a subject of criticism at home, approving a few things and condemning others. Thus the message of God to men is criticized and questioned, and made a subject of levity. What impressions are thus made upon the young by these careless, irreverent remarks the books of heaven alone will reveal. The children see and understand these things very much quicker than parents are apt to think. Their moral senses receive a wrong bias that time will never fully change. The parents mourn over the hardness of heart in their children and the difficulty in arousing their moral sensibility to answer to the claims of God. But the books of heavenly record trace with unerring pen the true cause. The parents were unconverted. They were not in harmony with heaven or with heaven's work. Their low, common ideas of the sacredness of the ministry and of the sanctuary of God were woven into the education of their children. It is a question whether anyone who has for years been under this blighting influence of home instruction will ever have a sensitive reverence and high regard for God's ministry and the agencies He has appointed for the salvation of souls. These things should be spoken of with reverence, with propriety of language, and with fine susceptibility, that you may reveal to all you associate with that you regard the message from God's servants as a message to you from God Himself.

Parents, be careful what example and what ideas you give your children. Their minds are plastic, and impressions are easily made. In regard to the service of the sanctuary, if the speaker has a blemish, be afraid to mention it. Talk only of the good work he is doing, of the good ideas he presented, which you should heed as coming through God's agent. It may be readily seen why children are so little impressed with the ministry of the word and why they have so little reverence for the house of God. Their education has been defective in this respect. Their parents need daily communion with God. Their own ideas need to be refined and ennobled; their lips need to be touched with a live coal from off the altar; then their habits, their practices at home, will make a good impression on the minds and characters of their children. The standard of religion will be greatly elevated. Such parents will do a great work for God. They will have less earthliness, less sensuality, and more refinement and fidelity at home. Life will be invested with a solemnity of which they have scarcely conceived. Nothing will be made common that pertains to the service and worship of God.

I am often pained as I enter the house where God is worshiped, to see the untidy dress of both men and women. If the heart and character were indicated by the outward apparel, then certainly nothing could be heavenly about them. They have no true idea of the order, the neatness, and the refined deportment that God requires of all who come into His presence to worship Him. What impressions do these things give to unbelievers and to the youth, who are keen to discern and to draw their conclusions?

In the minds of many there are no more sacred thoughts connected with the house of God than with the most common place. Some will enter the place of worship with their hats on, in soiled, dirty clothes. Such do not realize that they are to meet with God and holy angels. There should be a radical change in this matter all through our churches. Ministers themselves need to elevate their ideas, to have finer susceptibilities in regard to it. It is a feature of the work that has been sadly neglected. Because of the irreverence in attitude, dress, and deportment, and lack of a worshipful frame of mind, God has often turned His face away from those assembled for His worship.

Glossary of Liturgical Terms / C

Alleluia: (Hebrew, Hallelu-jah): an ascription to God from the ancient Hebrew liturgy.

Antiphon: A brief verse of a psalm or other text from Scripture which is sung or said.

Antiphonal: A method of singing between two parts of a choir, or between the choir and congregation.

Baptistry: That part of the church containing the tank for baptisms, and/or the tank itself.

Basilica: The early type of Christian church derived from the Roman hall used for legal or business purposes. It is usually rectangular with columns extending the length of the *nave* with a *narthex* at the entrance end.

Benediction: A declaration, usually by the minister or presiding elder, that announces the grace and care of God for the believing congregation. Most frequently the Aaronic form is used from Numbers 6: "The Lord bless you and keep you, the Lord make His face to shine upon you, and be gracious to you, the Lord lift up His countenance upon you, and give you peace; In the name of the Father, and of the Son, and of the Holy Spirit." Other benedictions that are often used are 2 Cor 13:14; Heb 13:20–21; Jude 24–25.

Bidding Prayer: A form of prayer that consists of a series of petitions, each composed of a request to pray for something special, a moment of silence for individual prayers, and a verbal prayer by the minister that incorporates the prayers of the congregation.

Chorale: A form of melody for the support of hymns used in the worship service of the church. Developed most artistically by J. S. Bach (1685–1750) for the organ.

Closing Prayer: A prayer offered in lieu of a *benediction* by the minister or presiding elder. Usually containing words of thanks for blessings received in worship and petitions for grace to be the church in the world for the next six days.

Constants: Those parts of the *order of service* which do not vary in intent from week to week.

Deacon: A member of the church ordained to various kinds of service in the church. During worship services deacons are in charge of receiving the offering and preparing for and assisting in the communion service.

Doxology: Means "blessing" and/or giving glory to God, such as: "Worthy is the lamb that was slain to receive power and riches and wisdom and might and honor and glory and blessing" (Rev 5:12). Another form can be the final verse of a hymn in which praise to the three Persons of the Trinity is sung.

Elder: Ordained members of the local church who, together with the pastor, exercise spiritual leadership and oversight. Qualifications for the office of elder are high (see Exod 18:21; Acts 6:3; 1 Tim 3:7; 2 Tim 2:2; 1 Tim 3:1–13; 4:12–16; Titus 2:1–8).

Eucharist: A Greek term meaning "thanksgiving," which was the ancient name for the celebration of the holy communion. Holy communion is a significant act of celebration and thanksgiving by the church.

Eucharistic Prayer: The prayer, or prayers, offered by presiding elders prior to the distribution of the bread and wine in communion. It should be noted that it is the congregation that needs to be dedicated so that the body of Christ can be broken bread and poured-out wine for the sake of Christ in the world.

Exposition: A method of explaining passages of Scripture through sermonizing.

Introit: The liturgical hymn at the beginning of worship. It is the entrance hymn of the service and announces, not the entrance of the minister and elders onto the platform, but the entrance of the whole congregation into the presence of God.

Invocation: A calling upon God at the beginning of a service, usually in the form, "In the name of the Father, and of the Son, and of the Holy Spirit," or some similar form.

Litany: A form of intercessory prayer with a marked responsive character, sometimes incorporating the singing of a choir.

Liturgy: From a Greek word meaning a "public work." The whole system of the services, rites, and ceremonies of the church, whether formal or informal. Sometimes referred to as the *order of service.*

Narthex: That portion of the church building comprising the entrance area for the congregation. In the ancient *basilica* it was called the porch and was open to the outside. It has since become an enclosed area, part of the church building proper.

Nave: That portion of the church building where the congregation sits during worship services.

Offertory: The action in the *liturgy* when the tithes and offerings are received from the congregation, usually accompanied by music by voice and/or instruments.

Occasional Service: A worship service of the congregation which does not occur on a regular basis, such as baptism, wedding, child dedication, and funeral.

Order of Service: Another term for *liturgy*, consisting of the ordered progression of worship activity to be engaged in by the congregation on any given occasion.

Opening Prayer: A prayer offered by the minister or elder in lieu of the invocation and inviting the presence of the Deity.

Ordinance: A term often used synonymously with "*sacrament*" to designate special celebrations such as the holy communion, foot-washing, and baptism.

Penitential Psalms: Those psalms that express a penitential spirit, such as 6, 32, 38, 51, 102, 130, 143. Thcy are used when it is desirable to lead the congregation into a confession of sin.

Pericope: A Greek term meaning a lesson from Scripture that is appointed for reading in public worship, and/or the basis for the day's sermon.

Responsive Reading: A reading from the Psalms or other portions of Scripture, sometimes printed in a special section in the hymnal and usually read responsively.

Ritual: Another term used synonymously with "*liturgy*" and "*order of service*," referring to the action of a congregation in worship.

Rubrics: A liturgical term used in reference to directions established by the church, or a local congregation, for the conduct of the services of that church. The name comes from the red ink that was usually used to distinguish such rules from other texts. It is synonymous with the term "rules." (See White, *Testimonies for the Church*, Vol. 5, p. 491.)

Sabbath: The seventh day of the week, Saturday, which God has sanctified and set aside for rest from labor and for corporate worship. Not to be confused with Sunday, the first day of the week.

Sacrament: A rite or *ordinance* of the church in which the focus is upon the receiving of God's gifts of grace, rather than on the sacrificial or giving aspects of worship, such as holy communion and baptism. In this sense prayer and the Sabbath can be thought of as sacramental.

Sanctus: Means "holy"; a verbal expression declaring the holiness of God and the Son, such as, "Holy, holy, holy, is the Lord God, the Almighty, who was and who is and who is to come" (Rev 4:8).

Sermon: The verbalizing of the Word of God, based on a biblical text or *pericope*.

Spirit of Prophecy: The term adopted by Seventh-day Adventists to refer to the counsel and the writings of Ellen G. White. (See Rev 19:10.)

Variants: Those parts of the *order of service* which vary in intent and/or content from week to week.

Vespers: A service for late afternoon or early evening. During the Reformation, vespers became the daily evening prayer service. Within the Seventh-day Adventist tradition it normally is held on Friday evening prior to sundown and/or on Saturday evening, and is used as a devotional and corporate means for opening and closing the Sabbath.

Bibliography

Allmen, J. J. von. *Preaching and Congregation.* Richmond, Va.: John Knox Press, 1962.

———. *Worship: Its Theology and Practice.* New York: Oxford University Press, 1965.

Bacchiocchi, Samuele. *Divine Rest for Human Restlessness.* Tesor Printing Co., 1980 (privately published).

Billington, Raymond J. *The Liturgical Movement and Methodism.* London: Epworth Press, 1969.

Bonhoeffer, Dietrich. *Life Together.* Trans. John W. Doberstein. New York: Harper and Bros., 1954.

———. *The Cost of Discipleship.* Trans. R. H. Fuller. New York: The Macmillan Co., 1957.

Borgen, Ole E. *John Wesley on the Sacraments.* Zurich: Publishing House of the United Methodist Church, 1972.

Brister, C. W. *Pastoral Care in the Church.* New York: Harper and Row Publishers, 1964.

Brunner, Emil. *Eternal Hope.* Philadelphia: Westminster Press, 1954.

Brunner, Peter. *Worship in the Name of Jesus.* St. Louis: Concordia Publishing House, 1968.

Burkhart, John E. *Worship.* Philadelphia: Westminster Press, 1982.

Calvin, John. *Institutes of the Christian Religion.* Ed. John T. McNeill. Trans. Ford Lewis Battles. Philadelphia: Westminster Press, 1960.

Coffen, Henry Sloan. *Communion Through Preaching.* New York: Scribner, 1952.

Delling, Gerhard. *Worship in the New Testament.* Philadelphia: Westminster Press, 1962.

Dunkle, William F., Jr., and Quillian, Joseph D., Jr. *Companion to the Book of Worship.* Nashville: Abingdon, 1970.

Eller, Vernard. *In Place of Sacraments.* Grand Rapids, Mich: William B. Eerdmans Publishing Co., 1972.

Eskew, Harry, and McElroth, Hugh T. *Sing With Understanding*. Nashville: Broadman Press, 1980.

Fant, Clyde E. *Bonhoeffer: Worldly Preaching*. Nashville: Thomas Nelson, Inc., 1975.

Green, Michael. *Evangelism in the Early Church*. Grand Rapids, Mich.: William B. Eerdmans Publishing Co., 1970.

Heppenstall, Edward. *Christ Our High Priest*. Washington: Review and Herald Publishing Association, 1972.

Heschel, Abraham. *The Sabbath*. New York: Farrar, Straus, and Young, 1951.

Holmes, C. Raymond. *It's a Two-Way Street*. Washington: Review and Herald Publishing Association, 1978.

Hoon, Paul Waitman. *The Integrity of Worship*. Nashville: Abingdon, 1971.

Oosterwal, Gottfried. *Mission Possible*. Nashville: Southern Publishing Association, 1972.

Paquier, Richard. *Dynamics of Worship*. Philadelphia: Fortress Press, 1967.

Pease, Norval. *And Worship Him*. Nashville: Southern Publishing Association, 1967.

Phifer, Kenneth G. *A Protestant Case for Liturgical Renewal*. Philadelphia: Westminster Press, 1965.

Rattenbury, J. Ernest. *The Eucharistic Hymns of John and Charles Wesley*. London: Epworth Press, 1948.

Rifkin, Jeremy, and Howard, Ted. *The Emerging Order*. New York: G. P. Putnam's Sons, 1979.

Segler, Franklin. *Christian Worship: Its Theology and Practice*. Nashville: Broadman Press, 1967.

Senn, Frank C. *Christian Worship: Its Cultural Setting*. Philadelphia: Fortress Press, 1983.

Seventh-day Adventist Bible Commentary. 10 vols. Ed. Francis D. Nichol. Washington: Review and Herald Publishing Association, 1957.

Shaughnessy, James, ed. *The Roots of Ritual*. Grand Rapids, Mich.: William B. Eerdmans Publishing Co., 1973.

Snyder, Howard A. *The Radical Wesley*. Downers Grove, Ill.: Inter-varsity Press, 1980.

Stratman, Gary D. *Pastoral Preaching*. Nashville: Abingdon, 1983.

Tappert, Theodore E., ed. *The Book of Concord*. Philadelphia: Fortress Press, 1959.

Tournier, Paul. *Guilt and Grace*. New York: Harper and Row, 1962.

______. *The Violence Within*. San Francisco: Harper and Row, 1978.

Turner, R. Edward. *Proclaiming the Word*. Berrien Springs, Mich.: Andrews University Press, 1980.

Wainwright, Geoffrey. *Eucharist and Eschatology*. New York: Oxford University Press, 1981.

Watson, David. *I Believe in the Church*. Grand Rapids, Mich.: William B. Eerdmans Publishing Co., 1978.

Webber, Robert E. *Worship Old and New*. Grand Rapids, Mich.: Zondervan, 1982.

White, Ellen G. *The Desire of Ages.* Mountain View, Calif.: Pacific Press Publishing Association, 1898.

———. *Patriarchs and Prophets.* Mountain View, Calif.: Pacific Press Publishing Association, 1958.

———. *Steps to Christ.* Mountain View, Calif.: Pacific Press Publishing Association, 1908.

———. *Testimonies for the Church.* 9 vols. Mountain View, Calif.: Pacific Press Publishing Association, 1948.

———. *The Adventist Home.* Nashville: Southern Publishing Association, 1952.

———. *Education.* Mountain View, Calif.: Pacific Press Publishing Association, 1903.

———. *Evangelism.* Washington: Review and Herald Publishing Association, 1946.

White, James F. *New Forms of Worship.* Nashville: Abingdon, 1971.

———. *Christian Worship in Transition.* Nashville: Abingdon, 1980.

———. *Introduction to Christian Worship.* Nashville: Abingdon, 1980.

———. *Sacraments as God's Self-Giving.* Nashville: Abingdon, 1983.

Willimon, William H. *Worship as Pastoral Care.* Nashville: Abingdon, 1979.

———. *The Service of God: How Worship and Ethics Are Related.* Nashville: Abingdon, 1983.